PILGRIMAGE TO PENTECOST

BY
PHILLIP BRASSFIELD

Carpenter's Son Publishing

Pilgrimage to Pentecost: Discovering the Passion, Purpose, and Power of Your Destiny

Copyright © 2012 by Phillip Brassfield

Published by Carpenter's Son Publishing, Franklin, Tennessee

Published in association with Larry Carpenter of Christian Book Services, LLC
www.christianbookservices.com

All Scripture quotations are taken from the New King James Version®. Copyright © 1982 by Thomas Nelson, Inc. Used by permission. All rights reserved.

Chart on Page 35 used by permission of Landon Galloway Mdiv.

Editor: Robert Irvin
Cover and Interior Layout Design: Suzanne Lawing

Printed in United States of America

978-0-9849771-0-9

ENDORSEMENTS

Dr. Phillip Brassfield is a brilliant bible scholar, an excellent communicator, and a personal friend of mine. He combines his in-depth knowledge of the scripture and a life-long walk with God to unfold this masterpiece of biblical truth. I can say confidently that he has a revelation on the subject and his passion for its application in our lives is obvious in every sentence. "Pilgrimage to Pentecost" inspired me to study the scripture more thoroughly and to pursue God with greater fervency. This book has the power to elevate a reader to a new plateau of understanding and relationship with God.

Bishop Randy Clark
Triumph Church
Sugarland, Texas

Every time I have a conversation with Phil Brassfield I walk away smarter and challenged. His passion for Christ and the Word is contagious. Phil has long been a preacher's preacher and a minister's friend. Now, with *Pilgrimage To Pentecost*, he has broken into the circle of 21st Century theologians and authors who are making a difference one reader at a time. I am a third generation Pentecostal minister. I cut my teeth on the pine wood pews of my dad's Pentecostal church. There's not much I haven't seen or experienced in the Spirit-filled movement. *Pilgrimage To Pentecost* has given me new revelation and insight on something that was never meant to be just an experience, but a lifestyle. Phil literally and figuratively takes Pentecost out of the Upper Room and shows how it fits in the every day challenges of life. I commend to you my dear friend's book.

Scott R. Jones
Senior Pastor – Grace Church –Houston, Texas
Chairman – Global Network of Christian Ministries

In October of 2011, I was in a Ministers' Conference in Phoenix, Arizona and heard Phil Brassfield preach on the subject "Pilgrimage to Pentecost." I don't remember when I have been so stirred in my spirit as that night. I quickly sought Phil out of the crowd and began to tell him of my delight with his message. Now, that material and more have been put in book form.

I am so happy about this book. Many people, ministers included, know little about their real destiny and what it takes to get there. I know Phil has a great book, but to me it is more than a book—it is a Journey to Destiny. The outpouring at Pentecost, for Israel and the new Church was a great destiny. But for us, with the Holy Spirit of God, we have only just begun. As you read this book, you will find yourself thinking backwards to your beginnings, and then you will learn more completely how to enjoy the journey to your ultimate destiny. This is the kind of book I like to give to my friends—and I will do just that.

Thank you Phil for your most excellent book and for the revelation of God to us as we read and enjoy what you have written.

Charles Green, Th. D.
President, Harvest Ministries to the World

Dr. Brassfield delivers a life-changing message for those who will drink in and apply the truths revealed in this book. Understanding is here to be found for the discerning and hungry. "Pilgrimage to Pentecost" is filled with powerful insights that can be directly and personally applied to your personal life and the life of the church.

Oren Paris III
President, Ecclesia College
Springdale, Arkansas

Having had the privilege to personally be associated with Dr. Phillip Brassfield for nearly 20 years, I assure you that this subject "Pilgrimage to Pentecost" has come out of a heart hungry for God. Dr. Brassfield has dedicated his life to God's service as he helps many hundreds find their destiny in Christ.

As you read each chapter of this book, you will find yourself on this journey, which is your personal pilgrimage to Pentecost. In the book Phil states that "being converted is much more than simply making a decision." To become a follower of Jesus we must make Him Lord of our lives by obeying and becoming a true follower, a disciple. Dr. Brassfield will help you make the journey, the pilgrimage to your own personal Pentecost.

Bishop Jabo' Green
Founding Pastor, Champion Life Centre
Spring, Texas

DEDICATION

I would like to dedicate this book to three men:

To my Grandfather, Rev. W.C. Pruett, who raised nine children and a farm, and served the Lord as a Minister of the Gospel for 60 years, planting churches, preaching revivals and loving the lost.

And to my dear Father, Dr. Rev. Leon Brassfield, who built and Pastored churches for 50 years, who walked with God in integrity and character, living "the life" before my young and impressionable eyes. You taught me to study the Word and to keep mine, to follow the Lord, live with integrity and love my family. You taught me to do what was right before God and man.

And to my big brother, Dr. Ken Brassfield, who was more like a dad to me than a brother, who also served God in Christian Ministry for over 20 years.

You have all finished your work here on earth and are with the Lord today, and I miss you desperately. But each of you had a part in the writing of this book. As I put words together to form sentences, paragraphs and chapters, I could hear your voices in the words and ideas that emerged. Your fingerprints are here, and clearly on my heart!

ACKNOWLEDGEMENTS

A very special thanks goes to my precious wife and best friend, Cathy, who has been a constant source of encouragement and support during our marriage and certainly the writing of this book. You always believed in me! I can feel it! Your love and consistent partnership has been an oasis of refreshment and safety for me. This is our book! We did it like everything else, together!

And to our wonderful staff:
Words can never express my deep gratitude for your dedication and support everyday, but especially during the many phases of development for this book.

To Jeannie Abbott, my Administrative Assistant and dear partner in all things ministry. You read this book until you almost had it memorized! Your attention to detail was a huge gift during this project, and every other day for that matter.

And to Amy Dew who kept the office running while we were sequestered for days of deliberation and focus on the project. Your help was critical to the process.

And to Landon Galloway, our resident scholar, who began as an Intern with Destiny years ago, went on to university returning with more degrees than the thermometer; and who helped with research and review, making sure that the material was as it should be!

CONTENTS

DISCOVERING YOUR DESTINY

Do you have a destiny? Do you believe that you were born for a reason, for a purpose? Most Christians do. But too often there is no one to warn us, or at least to help us fully grasp that, while pursuing our dreams we will face persistent challenges and constant struggles, not to mention disappointments.

Perhaps your destiny should come with a Caution label: "Warning: Aspiring to live a life of significance, and finding and fulfilling your purpose will require great endurance, unbelievable flexibility, and insane optimism." But even if your destiny did come with a warning, you should not be deterred. You can't live without purpose. It is your life!

What is *destiny* anyway? Well, it is different things to different people. Some would say that destiny is a place, that it is only discovered when you have arrived at your destination or goal. Others would say that it is really all about the process that gets you there. Most of those who truly find it would agree that it is both process and purpose, journey and destination. *But then there is a third component, perhaps the most important one. That is who we have become when we have arrived and survived the journey.* The fact is, as we travel and experience the process of the journey, we are changed. We become different people than the ones who began the trip—wiser, more balanced, more experienced people. We become people who have found our destinies. People who, because of the testing, trials, and tribulations of the process, are equipped to fulfill the purposes for which we have pressed on in the first place. Destiny, then, is part "where we are going," part "how we are getting there," and part "who we become" along the way.

> Destiny, then, is part "where we are going," part "how we are getting there," and part "who we become" along the way.

This book is about destiny. It is indeed about purpose and process, journey and destination. It is about the church collectively and the individuals who compose it. Both have a journey to experience and a goal to achieve. *Pilgrimage to Pentecost* is a gripping story about the journey and events leading to the destiny of the church and the everyday people who made the trip. And it is a destiny that continues to unfold to this day.

I believe Pentecost was—and is—God's destiny for the church as well as for the individual believer. Not in the doctrinal sense that you might imagine, but rather in that it was the birthday of a movement of believers that would be called the church. I also believe that the Day of Pentecost was the converging point of all of God's dealings with man from the beginning. It was as if all of the Old Testament events and characters, all of the covenants and prophecies, were aiming at one focal point in history, the day the church would be born and be released with power to fulfill the purpose of God. Pentecost would signal the birth of a mighty nation—a spiritual nation of people that is now emerging into its third millennium of existence. It would also ignite a divine fire that is destined to burn throughout eternity as God reveals his eternal purpose in the church.

Against the backdrop of biblical history and the first century, we will walk with Jesus and those who constituted the leadership of the first church as they journeyed toward the incredible life-changing release of power at Pentecost. This would become their defining moment.

Along the way we will examine the passion of the journey that was involved in the final days of Jesus' earthly ministry. We will no doubt identify with them and see ourselves and our lives as well, and hear the Master say, as his first followers heard, "If anyone desires to come after Me, let him deny himself, and take up his cross daily, and follow Me" (Luke 9:23).

Our journey toward destiny and Pentecost will involve a cross. As the story develops, this becomes abundantly clear. But the cross is not our final destiny, simply part of the journey, part of the process. *It is necessary, for it will help to make us what we must be if we are to know God's purpose for our lives completely.* There cannot be a Pentecost without a Calvary. And a Calvary is incomplete without a Pentecost. Often we have acted as if these two events were unrelated, as if they had little to do with one another. But we must realize that our journey of redemption that travels through Calvary is leading us to Pentecost. It moves from the passion of the Christ to the purpose of the church. This move will involve a pilgrimage, a journey no doubt filled with difficult moments and events that can shake the very foundations of who we are. But if we persevere, if we continue on, we will arrive at our Pentecost, our day of inheritance and empowerment. There we become new men and new women and, collectively, a new people, a new race. And from there we will be sent forth with destiny in our hearts and God's purpose as the focus of our objectives.

The journey that would lead to Pentecost and the genesis of this new race of mankind would begin with a struggle, a spiritual struggle. It would be a journey that would have its point of origin in the natural world through a covenant made between God and an earthly man named Abraham. This journey would travel a winding road of life and development through a people called the Jews and find its ultimate fulfillment in a new race of spiritual sons and daughters of God. The Jews would become the foundation for the introduction of a spiritual kingdom of people whose principle of life would not be limited to the natural realm. They would become a witness of and a launching point for God's revelation of this kingdom on earth.

The citizenship of this kingdom would not be based on an individual's natural origin, physical kinship to another person, geographical proximity to a city or region, or even ethnic similarity to others. Rather, it would be based on a spiritual reality—the reality of shared faith in Christ Jesus. But this nation would have a birthing point, and that would be the holy city of Jerusalem during a Jewish festival called Pentecost. This new nation would be called the church, the body of Christ, and its citizens called Christians.

The collective destiny of the church is one perspective that you will be exposed to in this book. But the interesting thing is that as we look at the events that led to that amazing moment and the people who were there, we will see ourselves in the crowd and realize that we, as Christians, are making the same journey in our time that they made in theirs. This will offer us a very personal perspective as well. While looking at one general picture in history we will see both viewpoints at once. From this picture we will examine God's destiny for the church but also see how that destiny works in the life of a believer. We will discover not only the purpose, but also the process, and how important both are to forming us into the individual people, and the church, that God had in mind when He imagined both. We will see that as we make the trip and arrive at our own personal Pentecost, our purpose individually, we will also discover the destiny that God has planned for all of us collectively. They are intertwined, intimately connected, and designed to be experienced as one!

Phil Brassfield

Heber Springs, Arkansas

February 2012

PART I

PART 1

Chapter One

THE WHERE ANSWERS THE WHY

Key Text: "When the Day of Pentecost had fully come, they were all with one accord in one place. And suddenly there came a sound from heaven, as of a rushing mighty wind, and it filled the whole house where they were sitting. Then there appeared to them divided tongues, as of fire, and *one* sat upon each of them. And they were all filled with the Holy Spirit and began to speak with other tongues, as the Spirit gave them utterance" (Acts 2:1-4).

Being raised in Pentecostal circles my entire life, I followed (for the most part) the commonly held view that the Upper Room was the location of the outpouring of the Holy Spirit on the Day of Pentecost. We were taught, essentially, that Jesus' disciples returned to Jerusalem and began a ten-day prayer meeting that eventually ushered in the outpouring of the Holy Spirit. I guess that's generally where we got the idea that you have to tarry, to wait on God, if we are to be filled with the Holy Spirit. We even had Scripture for it.

> *"Behold, I send the Promise of My Father upon you; but tarry in the city of Jerusalem until you are endued with power from on high" (Luke 24:49).*

So I've seen people hungry for more of God spend extensive amounts of time "tarrying," "seeking God," trying to figure out how to receive the free gift of God, the infilling of the Holy Spirit, that we believe is subsequent to the initial conversion experience. Taking this one verse alone, from our perspective, it would seem that the whole purpose of Pentecost was about power and that you had to tarry, or wait on God, to get it. This fit well into a works-based mentality that downplayed the grace of God and emphasized the responsibility of man in the process.

Now, before it sounds like I am about to take shots at the commonly held views of my faith tradition, let me say that I am thankful for my heritage. I have been taught so many wonderful things about God and the kingdom through our movement. It is the channel through which I came to faith in Christ. And I also want to affirm without reservation that I do believe in the fullness of the Holy Spirit working in the life of the believer. I believe that all of the spiritual gifts mentioned in Scripture are available for operation in the believer today, and that they function to both edify the believer personally and build up the church collectively. And I do believe that one of the side effects of a Spirit-filled life is supernatural power to give witness of the truth of Jesus Christ. That was clearly one of the dynamics that was present at the initial outpouring at Pentecost. But I also believe that we have not properly understood all of the events of that day and, because of this misunderstanding, we have missed the real wonder of the moment.

So, over years of indoctrination, as we focused on one dimension, the power of the outpouring, we interpreted the meaning of the Pentecostal event in the context of our presupposed theological ideas. In our preoccupation with the power of Pentecost, we have made it only about the experience of 120 believers in an obscure upper chamber in the city of Jerusalem and missed the greater purpose of God that precipitated the event in the first place. When you examine it a bit closer, without our traditional Pentecostal preconceived ideas, and look at what was achieved at Pentecost, there seems to be a much richer, broader meaning to what happened.

So to get to the real meaning of Pentecost, let's first look at the location of the outpouring. I believe that the "where" will answer the "why" and help us understand that first outpouring at a much deeper level.

Why the Temple Was the Likely Location

First, it is a general assumption among most Pentecostal and evangelical groups, for that matter, that the Holy Spirit fell in the Upper Room. This is probably because of the biblical references to the upper room in other New Testament passages such as Luke 22:12 and Mark 14:15, which speak of a common event, the upper room of the Lord's Supper; and Acts 1:13, which speaks of an upper room where the disciples of Jesus were staying during the Feast of Pentecost. It is logical, though not expressly indicated in Scripture, that this accommodation would have been one and the same place. And

> I believe that the "where" will answer the "why" and help us understand that first outpouring at a much deeper level.

there has been much speculation as to the relationship that Jesus and his disciples might have had with the particular owner of this upper room. Maybe it was a familiar place that they often used when visiting Jerusalem. Perhaps they rented it? Or it might have been simply loaned to them by a family member or friend. Jewish residents of Jerusalem would often offer hospitality to pilgrims who had come to Jerusalem for the three chief feasts of Israel. Whatever the case, we have traditionally assumed that it is there, in the Upper Room, that the Holy Spirit was poured out on that day. But does the Scripture actually say that? No!

Luke (author of the book of Acts) tells us in Acts chapter one that they return to Jerusalem, after Jesus' ascension to Heaven from the Mount of Olives, to the Upper Room "where they were staying" (Acts 1:13). While there, they conducted the business of replacing Judas' position of leadership with another of their number who had been faithful and had been with them since Jesus' baptism in water by John. We are also told that they continued in one mind and one accord.

> Whatever the case, we have traditionally assumed that it is there, in the Upper Room, that the Holy Spirit was poured out on that day. But does the Scripture actually say that?

But Luke uses a Hebraic-styled narrative break[1] to introduce chapter two and the events of chapter two. (It would later be divided as "chapter two," of course, but was not written originally by Luke as a "chapter two.") In other words, the events, and how Luke described them, changed the flow of the story and disconnected everything going on in chapter one from that of chapter two.

"When the Day of Pentecost had fully come, they were all with one accord in one place" (Acts 2:1).

This change lets the reader know that where the disciples were and what they were doing in chapter one is not necessarily where they were and what they were doing as chapter two opens.

Now let's remember that they are devout Jews. And this fact has to be accounted for in the story of Pentecost. **We must assume that they continued in their Jewish traditions after Jesus' ascension.** They did not understand, as of yet, the distinction that would develop between Judaism and Christianity. During feast times and regularly scheduled prayer times, they would have almost certainly followed their Jewish traditions. Luke tells us as he closes his gospel: "And they worshiped Him, and returned to Jerusalem with great joy, and were continually in the temple praising and blessing God. Amen" (Luke 24:52, 53). No doubt when it was time to pray they would have gone to the temple for their normal prayer times. We even see that evidenced later (Acts 3:1) when Peter and John encounter the lame man, begging, at the gate called Beautiful. He is healed in the encounter, but Luke tells us Peter and John were there to pray because it was prayer time, " . . . the hour of prayer, the ninth hour."

All of this understanding gives us a bit more insight into the Acts chapter two story. Being devout Jews and seeing that they demonstrated no apparent reason to reject the temple or their associated Jewish customs, we can safely ask: Where are they likely to have been when the "Day of Pentecost had fully come"?

Pentecost is the only one of Israel's chief feasts that was celebrated on a single day, as opposed to a week, or at least over several days. The doors of the temple opened just after midnight to allow the visiting crowds to have their sacrifices inspected by the priests. The services began with the morning sacrifices being offered and then prayer time followed around the third hour of the day, between 9 AM to 10 AM. Large numbers of pilgrims, perhaps tens of thousands,[2] would have been there, having traveled from all over the world. Luke even gives us a list of the different nationalities present (Acts 2:5-13).

It is unthinkable that the disciples would miss the morning ceremonies associated with the Feast of Pentecost. Indeed, it would have been disobedient to the command of the Lord from the Torah (Exodus 34:23, 24). So for them to have been in a neighborhood near, but not present at, the temple is not realistic.

Yes, the Scripture does say that the Spirit "filled the whole house where they were sitting" (Acts 2:2). But the house referred to was most likely the holy temple.

The Center for Holy Land Studies of the Assemblies of God suggests that, in Hebrew, the most common term used to refer to the temple is house. The Temple Mount is referred to as "the mountain of the house." Throughout the Gospel of Luke and Acts, Luke occasionally preserves Hebraic-styled syntax and idiom. His narrative mention of the "house" in which the disciples sat quite likely reflects this Hebrew idiom, referring to the holy temple, which is where one would expect to find Jesus' disciples during the festival of Pentecost, as well as the crowds they encounter.[3]

The Where Answers the Why

So to set this possibility in motion, let's imagine the scene. Tens of thousands of devoted Jews from all over the world have gathered for this grand one-day celebration that was both a celebration of the firstfruits of the wheat harvest and the commemoration of the giving of the law to Moses at Mt. Sinai. The sacrifices have been offered, sections of the Torah recited, and songs have been sung. The people have gathered in ethnic groups to read the Torah and pray.

It is at this point when, remarkably and suddenly, the place is shaken by the sound of a rushing, mighty wind. All the believers in Christ who were present, mostly from the regions of Galilee, begin to speak loudly, giving glory to God and testifying of his wonderful works. And they were speaking in the diverse native languages of the pilgrims who were present at the Feast. The people are amazed!

> The sacrifices have been offered, sections of the Torah recited, and songs have been sung. The people have gathered in ethnic groups to read the Torah and pray.

Peter the apostle stands to speak and explain what they are witnessing. Luke records his message for us (Acts 2:14-39). Peter explains that they are not drunk, as some had supposed, since it is the third hour of the day (prayer time, by the way)! Rather, he attributes the outpouring as the fulfillment of the prophet Joel. He then preaches the gospel of Jesus to them as a suffering Messiah and as a Savior who had been crucified and resurrected from the dead. At the end of his message about three thousand people respond to the gospel and are baptized. The only place in Jerusalem that could have accommodated that many hearing and being baptized was the temple, with its large outer court and ritual baths that were located at the southern entrance at the pilgrim's gate to the Temple Mount.[4]

Jewish Time Divisions and the Temple Sacrifices

The sacrificial system was at the heart of the temple ritual. Public and private offerings were made daily.

The hours in this chart are seasonal, so the length of the daylight hours varied with the season of the year. The Jewish daytime hours began with dawn and ended with sundown, which began the next day. The Romans began their day with the first hour at midnight and counted twelve hours, to noon, and then twelve more hours from noon to the next midnight. Today, we keep Roman time.

SCHEDULE OF THE HOURS OF PRAYER AND THE TEMPLE LITURGICAL SERVICE

JEWISH TIME	ROMAN TIME
FIRST HOUR After the chief priest prepares the altar (Leviticus 1:7; 6:1-6, 8-13; *Mishnah: Tamid* 1:2), the first male lamb of the Tamid (daily) sacrifice is brought out and tied to the altar at dawn (*Mishnah: Tamid* 3:2, 3:3).	**DAWN** The twice-daily communal sacrifice of the Tamid is the focus of religious life for the covenant people (Exodus 29:38-42; Numbers 28:4-8). It is the only sacrifice other than the Feast of Firstfruits or the Sabbath that requires a single male lamb for the liturgical service. The Sabbath requires a male lamb *in addition* to the Tamid lamb for each of the two Sabbath services (Numbers 28:9, 10).
SECOND HOUR	**8-9 AM**
THIRD HOUR The first Tamid lamb is sacrificed (*Mishnah: Tamid* 3:7).	**9-10 AM** The Temple gates open for the communal "Shacharit" (morning) prayer service (Acts 2:15) at the start of the third hour. Individual morning prayers may be recited until noon (Mishnah 4:1).

FOURTH HOUR	10-11 AM
FIFTH HOUR	11-NOON
SIXTH HOUR The second lamb is brought out and tied to the altar at high noon *(Mishnah: Tamid 4:1)*.	NOON-1 PM The second Tamid lamb is given a drink from a gold cup and is tied to the altar until the time of sacrifice.
SEVENTH HOUR	1-2 PM
EIGHTH HOUR	2-3 PM
NINTH HOUR The second Tamid lamb is sacrificed (*Antiquities of the Jews* 14.4.3 [65]); Philo, *Special Laws* I, XXXV [169]).	3-4 PM 3 PM is the second hour of prayer (Acts 3:1; 10:9) and the "*Minchah*" (gift-offering); also called the hour of confession.
TENTH HOUR	4-5 PM
ELEVENTH HOUR	5-6 PM
TWELVETH HOUR	6 PM-SUNDOWN

Further: Notice that according to St. Mark's Gospel, Jesus went to the cross at the third hour, which in Jewish time corresponds to our 9 AM (Mark 15:25), and according to the Gospel accounts, he gave up his life at the ninth hour, our 3 PM.

The Jewish day began at sundown. The daytime was divided into twelve seasonal hours, but the day's division of hours was focused on the schedule of the Tamid sacrifice.

© Michal E. Hunt 1991, revised 2012

Source: www.AgapeBibleStudy.com

When we settle in our mind that the most likely *place* for the outpouring was the Jewish temple and that God had purposely orchestrated the place and the time with careful planning, I believe it helps us understand the *why*. And the why was so much greater than just the experience of power received by 120 gathered in an obscure upper room. It was, in a single moment, to ignite a movement around the world, as people were undoubtedly converted from all over the world at that one great event. It is as if God planned this moment to assist the fledgling disciples who had just received the Great Commission to take the good news all over the world to every creature.

> When we settle in our mind that the most likely *place* for the outpouring was the Jewish temple and that God had purposely orchestrated the place and the time with careful planning, I believe it helps us understand the *why*.

Pentecost was God's sovereign way to override racial prejudice, ethnic barriers, gender issues, and the natural resentment that the disciples must have felt toward the people of Jerusalem who had just participated in Jesus' crucifixion. When many of them came to faith as a result of the work of the Holy Spirit, all questions were answered. Forgiveness was for everyone—even those who had participated in his death—and every person from any country who called on the name of the Lord could be saved.

So we can see that the *where* truly answers the why.

Impact Points

1. **The location of the outpouring of the Holy Spirit is important because it provides us a glimpse into the purpose of God for the church.** God's purpose was to birth his church and ignite a global movement in one miraculous moment.

Acts 2:5, 11: "And there were dwelling in Jerusalem Jews, devout men, from every nation under heaven. . . . we hear them speaking in our own tongues the wonderful works of God."

2. **By connecting the power of the Holy Spirit in the life of the believer to the purpose of God in the world,** we learn that in the kingdom of God power must always have a redemptive purpose.

Acts 1:8: "But you shall receive power when the Holy Spirit has come upon you; and you shall be witnesses to Me in Jerusalem, and in all Judea and Samaria, and to the end of the earth."

For Group Discussion or Self-Reflection

Power is perhaps the most sought after—and, sadly, abused—characteristic in humanity. But power for power's sake is almost always used to exploit others for selfish intentions. Describe your view(s) of power and some of your experiences with it, both in a positive and negative sense.

Coaching for Success

Power in the kingdom of God will always have a redemptive purpose. Jesus told his disciples that they would receive power after the Holy Spirit had come upon them (Acts 1). Many Christians have interpreted that to imply some kind of supernatural physical force or magical ability. And the Holy Spirit surely does enable us to do things we could not normally do through the gifts of the Spirit. But whatever the expression of the power of the Holy Spirit, that power will always be intended to perform the will of God through the life of the believer for the benefit of the mission of the church.

Don't seek power for power's sake or to make a name for yourself; seek the will of God to be done in and through you. Ask for his supernatural influence and grace to enable you to courageously stand for him in a wicked generation and to effectively witness of his truth and love to all who will listen.

Prayer of Reflection

Dear Lord, I know that you have a great purpose for my life and that if I am to know and experience that purpose I need power. But help me to always remember that your power is released in me for your will to be accomplished in and through my life. Today I seek you! I seek your will for my life and the world I live in. I trust you to grant me the power that I need to accomplish your will when and where I need it. Holy Spirit, I invite you to fill me not only with your power but also with your purpose, because I know that it's only in your purpose that I find peace and satisfaction. I believe that as I am increasingly surrendered to you and your plan I become a greater channel for your power to flow into my world.

PART II

Chapter Two

GOD'S STRATEGIC PLAN

Key Text: "And we know that all things work together for good to those who love God, to those who are the called according to His purpose" (Romans 8:28).

Probably more than any other day recorded in Scripture, the Day of Pentecost carries with it a rare mystique and lure of hope. For it was much more than a day when the gifts of the Spirit would be demonstrated with power, though it was certainly that. It was the beginning of something wonderful, powerful—the beginning of a movement that would be the vanguard and facilitator of the consummation of the ages. It was a day when a great harvest would begin, one that would be inaugurated and affirmed to the world, a harvest whose firstfruits would be offered in the temple to God and before the people with undeniable majesty and power.

Often called the birthday of the church, Pentecost was an annual Jewish festival, also known as the Feast of Weeks. It was one of Israel's three chief feasts; each required all Jewish men to visit Jerusalem. It was celebrated seven weeks and a day (or fifty days) after the Passover. This is where the word *Pentecost* comes from. The word simply means fifty.

Israel's Annual Feasts: A Closer Look

Feast	Feast Our Corresponding Month	Scripture References	Significance
The Feast of Passover	March-April	Exodus 12:1-4; Leviticus 23:5; Numbers 9:1-14, 28:16; Deuteronomy 16:1-7	Commemorated the Hebrews' deliverance from Egypt
The Feast of Unleavened Bread	March-April	Exodus 12:15-20, 13:2-10; Leviticus 23:6-8; Numbers 28:17-25; Deuteronomy 16:3, 4, 8	Indicated the beginning of the barley harvest
The Feast of Firstfruits	March-April	Leviticus 23:9-14; Numbers 28:26	Celebration of the Firstfruits of the barley harvest
The Feast of Weeks (Pentecost)	May-June	Exodus 23:16, 34:22; Leviticus 23:15; Numbers 28:26-31; Deuteronomy 16:9-12	Indicated the end of the wheat harvest
The Feast of Trumpets	September-October	Leviticus 23:23-25; Numbers 29:1-6	Day of special offerings accompanied by trumpet blasts
Day of Atonement (Yom Kippur)	September-October	Leviticus 16, 23:23-25; Numbers 29:7-11	Solemn day when high priest offered sacrifice to atone for Israel's sin
The Feast of Tabernacles	September-October	Exodus 23:16, 34:22; Leviticus 23:33-36, 39-43	Indicated the beginning of the agricultural year

Landon Galloway MDiv

It is fitting that Jerusalem should be the location for the outpouring of God's Spirit. This city had been pivotal throughout Jewish history. It was in the area associated with Jerusalem that Abraham had offered Isaac to God, David had established his kingdom, and Solomon had built his famed temple. David and Solomon's kingdom periods were Israel's gilded age, indeed, but

> It is fitting that Jerusalem should be the location for the outpouring of God's Spirit.

there were some interesting similarities between the Jerusalem of Jesus' day and that of Solomon's. Jerusalem was the capital of Israel during the reigns of David and Solomon, as it was in Jesus' time, and Herod, the king during Jesus' time, was the first Jewish king to rule a united kingdom of Israel since Solomon. Palaces and architectural monuments had also returned to prominence during Herod's time, as they were in Solomon's day. Solomon had built the first temple that Israel would enjoy; Herod built the last. There was also a flow of prosperity in Israel during Herod's reign that had not been since Solomonic times.

But Jerusalem occupied a special place in the mind of God as well, even a spiritual place. From the beginning of Israel's Kingdom Age, God had chosen Jerusalem as a place of relationship and agreement. It was Jerusalem that God had chosen to identify with his name. During the dedication of Solomon's Temple, the concept of both Jerusalem and the temple being associated with the name of God is emphasized again and again. It is mentioned no less than thirteen times during Solomon's dedication.

Solomon's Address: the Blessings During the Dedication of the Temple

2 Chronicles 6:3: "Then the king turned around and blessed the whole assembly of Israel, while all the assembly of Israel was standing."

2 Chronicles 6:4: "And he said: 'Blessed be the LORD God of Israel, who has fulfilled with His hands what He spoke with His mouth to my father David, saying,'"

> *2 Chronicles 6:5:* "'Since the day that I brought My people out of the land of Egypt, I have chosen no city from any tribe of Israel in which to build a house, that My name might be there, nor did I choose any man to be a ruler over My people Israel.'"
>
> *2 Chronicles 6:6:* "'Yet I have chosen Jerusalem, that My name may be there, and I have chosen David to be over My people Israel.'"
>
> *2 Chronicles 6:7:* "'Now it was in the heart of my father David to build a temple for the name of the LORD God of Israel.'"
>
> *2 Chronicles 6:8* "'But the LORD said to my father David, 'Whereas it was in your heart to build a temple for My name, you did well in that it was in your heart.'"
>
> *2 Chronicles 6:9:* "'Nevertheless you shall not build the temple, but your son who will come from your body, he shall build the temple for My name.'"

With God, the application of his name normally has to do with covenant. So we see that Jerusalem was always viewed as a place of covenant. ***Therefore, many of the covenant concepts that we speak about today in the New Testament had their origins in this very special holy city.***

It seems only fitting that the Lord would send his disciples back to Jerusalem for the coming of the greatest of all promises. The fact that the Holy Spirit's outpouring and its resulting mission was the destiny of the church and was first poured out in Jerusalem connects all that the law and the prophets had spoken in the Old Testament to that which Jesus spoke and fulfilled during his life. It was imperative that God connect all that was recorded and prophesied previously in the Old Testament with this new movement in one seamless flow of divine purpose, synthesized in this one strategic event—Pentecost.

If this is true and if God meticulously planned the birth of the church from the foundation of the world (see Ephesians 1:4, 5), then he clearly has the knowledge, capability, and foresight to plan a destiny for us all. I wish I could always remember that. Sometimes it is easy to forget when you are living your life a second at a time without knowing what tomorrow holds, and without an easy-to-understand "how to" manual. (I don't know about yours, but my life did not come with one of those.) So the idea that there is a supreme—and benevolent—Being who has a plan for my life and is working that plan toward my greatest good is a challenging one for me to accept. But it's true. But when I look, I can see that the events of my life and the way things have happened to bring me to where I am today demonstrate this. And that is exactly what the Bible teaches as well, that God has a destiny for us all.

> When I look, I can see that the events of my life and the way things have happened to bring me to where I am today demonstrate this. And that is exactly what the Bible teaches as well, that God has a destiny for us all.

Destiny: God's Plan and Purpose

For a moment, let's focus on this idea of destiny. To believe in destiny, we have to adhere to the idea that God is "all knowing," which includes foreknowledge, and that he is also a personal being who has a plan for our lives. We must accept that, from the moment we are born, he is effectively working and adjusting the events of our lives to lead us into our destinies. The idea of destiny in Scripture is one that makes its appearance often. In the Old Testament we see a picture of a God who pronounces blessing or judgment in advance, often generations before it comes to pass. The whole concept of a prophet implies a God-ordained intention and awareness of future events. Scripture is packed with story after story of how God worked miracles in the lives of people, made kingdoms to rise and to fall, and got involved in many other creative ways in the lives of people to lead them into their divine purposes.

There is probably no greater example in all of Scripture of just such divine awareness and intervention than that of Queen Esther. She was an orphan Jewess, striking in beauty, who was reared by her cousin, Mordecai. She would become the driving force behind the preservation of the Jews from ruin during the reign of Ahasuerus the Persian in the fifth century B.C. He is believed to be King Xerxes I, who succeeded Darius I, in 485 B.C., and ruled for about twenty years over 127 provinces from India to Ethiopia. Wielding absolute power, he held the future of the Jews in his hands. But God used him to achieve his purposes through the influence of Esther. While she was the most unlikely of people, she was placed in Ahasuerus' kingdom by God at a strategic time. Aided by her remarkable beauty and grace, she influenced King Ahasuerus to grant favor for and show kindness and protection to the Jews. She also demonstrated great wisdom and patience while being coached by Mordecai as to the best possible time to reveal her own Jewish identity and the burden she carried for her people. What mighty armies could not do, and diplomatic envoys would have failed to accomplish, a young Jewess, with a passion and an awareness of her purpose, achieved. And an entire nation was preserved and blessed as a result. All this was her destiny.

And we could go on and on from individual to individual with the essential story line being the same and the underlying principles being consistent. We could speak of Moses and Joseph, of Gideon and David, each one unique in their own way, yet used by God to fulfill his purpose. Each was led through a pilgrimage for a purpose, leading to a destiny.

And as it was with each of them, so it was with the birth of the church. God clearly had a plan at work to bring the church into existence. The location, the manner, the timing, and those involved on the day of Pentecost clearly demonstrate divine design and sovereign intent.

How wonderful it is when we realize that we do indeed serve a God who loves us with such a deep love and compassion. And that his awareness of our potential, both positive and negative, is so complete that he can plan our future being attentive to even the most minute of details. He has the capacity to take the difficult moments of our lives, our bad decisions, accidental mistakes, and even the evil intentions of others, and use them as a catalyst for producing his purposes in our lives. The apostle Paul echoes this belief in numerous occasions in Scripture, not the least of which is the famed passage in Romans 8:28:

> *"And we know that all things work together for good to those who love God, to those who are the called according to His purpose."*

Life then becomes a journey into that purpose, and it would seem that we all are on that voyage, saint and sinner alike. Now, I'm not saying that we have no choice, nor am I preaching predestination. There is a difference between "foreknowledge" and "causing to be." I'm talking about a God who has a righteous ability to orchestrate the events of our lives, good and bad, into a force that can propel us into our destinies if we will allow him.

God placed an innate desire to know and live our destiny in all of mankind. This quest often involves a hunger to know who we are and to understand why we are here. These are age-old questions that have been asked since the dawn of time. The inner belief in most of us that life has meaning, and man's search for that meaning, has been a great catalyst for achievement throughout history. In an attempt to answer these questions, exploration, discovery, and social transitions have taken place. Seeking one's purpose, being allured by the quest to not only know, but to experience one's destiny to the fullest, must be ranked among the greatest needs a person can have in the human experience.

It could be argued that this sense of destiny is a component of the character of God, deposited by God himself into man at creation. After all, man was created in the image of God, according to his likeness. Our destiny, and the satisfaction of knowing that destiny, is hidden in God and experienced through our awareness of him and willingness to build a relationship with him. Being omniscient, God is intimately acquainted with our lives and our potential. The psalmist makes this point when he says:

> "O Lord, You have searched me and known me. You know my sitting down and my rising up; You understand my thought afar off. You comprehend my path and my lying down, and are acquainted with all my ways. For there is not a word on my tongue, but behold, O Lord, You know it altogether. You have hedged me behind and before, and laid Your hand upon me. Such knowledge is too wonderful for me; it is high, I cannot attain it. . . . Your eyes saw my substance, being yet unformed. And in Your book they all were written, The days fashioned for me, When as yet there were none of them" (Psalm 139:1-6, 16).

Here the writer tells us that even before we were born God had seen all of our days. This is possible because of the vantage point from which God views our lives. God is eternal—he is without beginning or end. For us, eternity is a concept that is beyond our ability to comprehend. We associate eternity with time—a really long amount of time. But actually, eternity is not a long time. It is no time. God is not limited by time. He created time when he put the universe in motion.

We must conclude that God is here now, is already in tomorrow, and has remained a constant presence throughout history.

And before the universe was, God was. Thus, we must conclude that God is here now, is already in tomorrow, and has remained a constant presence throughout history.

Romans 8:28 tells us that God is not only present but also active in the lives of those who love him. Earlier in the passage the writer tells us that it's the Holy Spirit who becomes the spiritual radar leading us into God's plan for our lives. This work is accomplished by aligning our prayers with the will of God.

> *"Likewise the Spirit also helps in our weaknesses. For we do not know what we should pray for as we ought, but the Spirit Himself makes intercession for us with groanings which cannot be uttered. Now He who searches the hearts knows what the mind of the Spirit is, because He makes intercession for the saints according to the will of God" (Romans 8:26, 27).*

The Holy Spirit is actively working in us to guide us into God's will for our lives (our destiny). Thus, we can never truly realize our destiny until we are led by the Spirit into what Paul calls, in the Greek, the prothesis of God.

> *"And we know that all things work together for good to those who love God, to those who are the called according to His purpose" (Romans 8:28).*

The word purpose is "prothesis" in the Greek.[5] The prefix *pro* means "before." The word *thesis* means "a place" or a particular position. Hence, students write thesis papers in college. The paper is their position on a particular subject. In Romans 8, Paul is saying that the Holy Spirit is not only aligning us with the will of God in our hearts, but also causing the events of our lives to work together (the word *work* is 'sunergeo', in the Greek. It means to synergize forces together) for the realization of his purpose in our lives.

You see, we all have a destiny, and God is committed to that purpose. Paul calls it, in Romans 12:2, "That good and acceptable and perfect will of

God." But this purpose involves a process. It involves a shift, a move out of one thing and into a new thing. For most of us the shift into our destiny is not a single giant step, but rather a series of smaller moves and experiences that lead us from one season of our lives into another. This process can be seen even in the life of our Lord Jesus and in the development of the church. While Pentecost was and is the destiny of the church, the process began much earlier and there were several steps. But we must understand that God was working through these steps to lead the church where he wanted her to be and to become what he wanted her to become. Sure, at certain times and in certain points in history it may have looked as if God had abandoned his church—but he never has. Rather, he has allowed her to endure the developmental process that we all must travel through. It is a process that involves change, refinement, and even crisis—and one that prepares us for our destiny.

Impact Points

1. **The desire to know and experience your destiny is a part of God's divine design for your life.** This destiny is your purpose in life, and only knowing and experiencing it can satisfy the inner longing for significance that we all have inside.

   Psalms 139:16, 17: "Your eyes saw my substance, being yet unformed. And in Your book they all were written, The days fashioned for me, When *as yet there were* none of them. How precious also are Your thoughts to me, O God! How great is the sum of them!"

2. **God has a plan for your life.** Therefore, do not step out of faith when difficult events take place. God is in control of your life if you will walk by faith with him. Accept this reality: God is not passive about nor disinterested in your future, but is aggressively at work through the events of your life to keep you on course with his plan.

   Philippians 2:13: "For it is God who works in you both to will and to do for His good pleasure."

3. **Surrender to the fact that God knows what is best for you and that he has a righteous ability to synergize (*sunergeo*, from the Greek) the events of our lives—good and bad—into a force that can propel us into our destiny.**

   Philippians 1:6: "Being confident of this very thing, that He who has begun a good work in you will complete it until the day of Jesus Christ."

For Group Discussion or Self-Reflection

Take a moment and think about your life, where you are now in relationship to what you have always dreamed of doing or becoming. There is a gap, right? Discuss what you can do to narrow the gap between your current reality and your dream. For example: list the relationships, personal skills, education, and personal disciplines that you might need to develop if you are to achieve your goals. Now, before you move forward, stop and ask God what he has planned for your life and then record your thoughts.

Coaching for Success

There are clues to God's plans for our lives that are hidden in the passions, gifts, and talents that we possess, as well as in the dreams that fill our hearts. God placed them in us for his purposes. Understanding, cataloging, and developing these things can greatly enhance our abilities and potential to achieve our goals and dreams. Carefully list and assess the things in your life that you believe are gifts from God and which of them that you need to develop further.

Prayer of Reflection

Lord, let me see my life through your eyes, from your wise and loving perspective. My vision is too often clouded by my own perceived limitations as well as the situations and circumstances of my life, and I need your help to break out of the limiting patterns of life and find my way into the future that you have planned for me. I believe that you have a plan at work. Lead me into your perfect will and purpose for my life, and give me the courage to act as you lead the way.

Chapter Three

DESTINY

Key Text: Matthew 3:1-3: "In those days John the Baptist came preaching in the wilderness of Judea, and saying, 'Repent, for the kingdom of heaven is at hand!' For this is he who was spoken of by the prophet Isaiah, saying: 'The voice of one crying in the wilderness: "Prepare the way of the Lord; Make His paths straight."'"

There is a stage in the process of nuclear fission called critical mass. Now, let me preface my thoughts by saying that what I know about nuclear fission you could write on the head of a pin with a magic marker, but I was intrigued when I stumbled onto this interesting phrase. Like most speakers, I am always on the lookout for catchy titles and vivid illustrations, titles to which people can relate. So you can imagine that when I heard the phrase "critical mass," it got my immediate attention. Upon closer examination it seems that this phrase is the name for the stage in the process of fission where the atom reaches a point that it can no longer remain what it has always been. It is the stage just before it splits, multiplies, and then releases its power. As I understand it, a force from outside the atom has created so much pressure on the atom that it literally begins to alter the atomic structure until it reaches this final stage before fission occurs—the stage called critical mass.[6]

While this whole process moves from stage to stage, one step at a time, a sudden moment occurs where fission takes place. In the foundry where iron ore is heated until it becomes a liquid and then is poured into a mold to make building materials, this point in time is called the molten moment. In both cases there is a process followed by a specific moment where transformation takes place, potential is released, and a new purpose is achieved. But the arrival of this new purpose does not come without great trauma for both the atom and the ore. So it is with the development of us as believers, and the church collectively, as we journey toward our destinies. The process involves our own "molten moments" and circumstances that bring us to our own points of "critical mass." There is, it would seem, an extreme price to be paid for experiencing your destiny. It almost always involves a long and winding road filled with change, trauma, and resistance.

Having coached and assisted countless Christians in navigating the journeys toward their destinies, I have discovered this over and over again. I have come to believe that as surely as the atom contains one of the most powerful forces of the universe, God has also invested the potential for greatness in the lives of those whom he has called. This potential, like the atom, contains all the power and resource needed to achieve, fulfill, and become God's agents for change in this world. But for this force to be released there must be a breaking, a crushing, a splitting of our lives. Before we are released into God's purpose, we must be transformed through the fire of the process that leads us through the stages, steps, and brokenness associated with our journey. It's been said that God wants his glory to shine through us—but first must break us so that glory can be

> I have come to believe that as surely as the atom contains one of the most powerful forces of the universe, God has also invested the potential for greatness in the lives of those whom he has called.

released. These moments of brokenness surely lead us to a sudden moment when we release what is inside—when we become, when we are empowered and transformed.

With this idea in mind, I was drawn to a passage of Scripture where a different, yet just as critical, moment is recorded.

> *"When the day of Pentecost had fully come, they were all with one accord in one place. And suddenly there came a sound from heaven, as of a rushing mighty wind, and it filled the whole house where they were sitting" (Acts 2:1, 2).*

Without a doubt, the Day of Pentecost is one of the watershed moments in all of Jewish and Christian history. *For this sudden moment was one that would change the flow of history, alter contemporary religious ideas, and forge a newness and realism that was not present in the Jewish religious system of that day.* Pentecost was the culmination of generations of traumatic moments, experiences, prophesies, and promises in the lives of God's people. But it was also the genesis of Christianity. On the Day of Pentecost God would birth the church through the mother of Judaism, via the person of Jesus Christ. This moment would blend the revelation of the God of the Old Testament with the person of Jesus Christ and reveal a powerful new spiritual revelation and reality called the church.

Pentecost. It was when formal religion and spirituality would take a quantum leap upward and forward. It was the birthday of the church and the destiny of the believer. *It would be the moment of history that would transform a ragtag mob of zealots, fishermen, ex-prostitutes, and priests into a movement that would shake the world, subdue kingdoms, and cover the earth in a single generation.*

As with atomic fission, there were stages and steps leading to this moment of Pentecost. There was a process with tremendous pressure being placed upon the atom of God's people throughout history. The pressure had begun as far back as when God had promised a Redeemer who would right the wrongs initiated in the Garden of Eden by Adam and Eve, and reverse the curse that resulted from their sin. (Read Genesis chapter 3 for the entirety of this account.) From that beginning, one can examine a multitude of moments of crisis with growing intensities as good conflicted with evil, and as God powerfully draws his people toward his preplanned purpose for them. These characters' lives and stories appear on the timeline of history as it races toward the arrival of God's promised Redeemer. As the pressure increased with each subsequent event and upon each character, it portrays an incredible drama teaching us the lessons that process and change are part of the development of our lives and destinies. Every strategic moment and each biblical character represents a series of events that constructs a road leading out of the status quo into a new future and toward ultimate destinies.

While the characters and events leading to Pentecost were no different than those who had gone before, their season was. For the season was the one that would witness the arrival of the prophesied Redeemer who was the Jewish Messiah, the critical mass of Judaism, and its molten moment—Pentecost, the birth and destiny of the church.

As I've discussed this process, *I know that for most of us, our lives have been a process, a journey, moving from one stage to another and not without crisis.* Crisis? Oh yes, we've experienced plenty of them—defining moments when we reached critical mass, moments when the fire grew so hot that we melted and were transformed. In these moments, the greatness that God has deposited within us is revealed.

A story that demonstrates this as well as any I have ever heard is recorded in Chuck Colson's book *The Body*. The book is an excellent witness to the impact that the church of Europe had in the process of reform that led to the fall of the Iron Curtain and the demise of communism in Eastern Europe. In the book, Colson relates a powerful story of a young pastor named Laszlo Tokes in Timisoara, Romania. Tokes, through a strange set of circumstances, became pastor of the local Hungarian Reformed Church in Timisoara in 1987. And it would not be long until this young man would experience his very own critical mass. Laszlo had a great passion for God and the things of God. Even amidst the cold, atheistic bondage that was so prevalent during the communist regime of Nicolae Ceausescu, this young man was consumed with passion for God and knew that he had a destiny. He brought freshness to the pulpit that was filled with Holy Spirit power, and before long the little crowds of only a few had swelled to more than five thousand.

Of course, this drew the attention of the communist government, and the season of brokenness that followed for Laszlo and his young family was brutal as they were relentlessly persecuted by the secret police. Beaten repeatedly and threatened with death, he preached on until the secret police delivered the final message that led them to the critical mass of their lives and ministries, a true molten moment: "Stop your preaching or we will exile you to a remote farm with no phone, electricity, or connection to this town or the people of this town." They gave them a Friday deadline, which was December 15, 1987. As the moment approached, the young pastor and his wife went into the church sanctuary that represented the God and the congregation that they loved so much. Laszlo wrapped himself in his clerical robes and waited near the communion table. To Laszlo and his wife's surprise, the congregation surrounded the church in support of their pastors. And as the secret police began a siege of the church compound, the crowds of supporters grew and grew until the eyes of a nation were fixed on the Hungarian Reformed Church of Timisoara. That moment of crisis was the beginning of what is now called the famed "six days in December." Those six days in December would be the critical mass not only for Laszlo and Edith, but also for freedom in Romania. It would become the fission of a new, free nation. As the secret police stormed the church, thronging crowds began to sing "Awake Romania." And awake they did. The crowds then turned and began to march toward the capitol. Thousands turned into tens of thousands, and while hundreds died in a hail of gunfire, the nation's passion for freedom grew until it could not be stopped. Within six days the Ceausescu government was gone (the Ceausescus were executed, following a hasty show trial, on December 21) and freedom was ringing over an awakened Romania.[7]

> He preached on until the secret police delivered the final message that led them to the critical mass of their lives and ministries, a true molten moment

While our own seasons of brokenness and crisis may have been less dramatic than those of Laszlo and Edith, we have all had them. Every road to destiny has them. And though these moments are uncomfortable, even painful, they are necessary. They stand between you and your destiny. Critical mass always comes before fission. *Crisis is the midwife that assists in the birthing of your future.* It is the final step that will lead toward your fission into something different, into someone who you have never been before and certainly never thought that you could become. These moments are your rites of passage, your badges of courage, and are the necessary guideposts that mark your course along life's road as you make your pilgrimage into a life of significance.

God has a destiny for you. But don't be surprised when it involves a fission process and molten moments. These moments will transform you and send you on a journey toward something new, perhaps a Pilgrimage to Pentecost.

* * * * *

In our next chapter we will begin to discuss certain steps that led to the destiny of the church. Time would not allow us to examine them all, but we will focus on the emergence of the ministry of John the Baptist and the arrival of the prophesied Redeemer, Jesus Christ, and how these events affected the environment of their day. Certainly the arrival and subsequent messages of these men began to alter the molecular structure of the Jewish faith, pushing the movement toward crisis. It was a crisis that would give birth to Christianity. But before the fission of Judaism that produced the emergence of Christianity would come the critical mass of redemption.

Impact Points

1. **Each of us experiences challenges in moments when we are broken by difficult situations and circumstances.** They are our points of critical mass, our "molten moments." These moments can push us to our breaking points. But they are extremely important to our development as individuals! As with the atom, our true strength and energy, what is really inside of us, is only released after we have endured the trauma and pressure that produces change.

   2 Corinthians 12:9: "And He said to me, 'My grace is sufficient for you, for My strength is made perfect in weakness.'"

2. **God's plan for us involves more than just a single discovery moment. It involves a process with stages and steps.** It is more like a journey than a single event.

   Psalm 25:4: "Show me Your ways, O LORD; Teach me Your paths."

3. **When broken by the circumstances of life, we have to make a choice.** Do we let the pain of the situation cause us to become bitter or better? Our perspective, the way we view the process, really defines our potential.

   1 Samuel 30:6: "Now David was greatly distressed, for the people spoke of stoning him, because the soul of all the people was grieved, every man for his sons and his daughters. But David strengthened himself in the LORD his God."

For Group Discussion or Self-Reflection

List several experiences that have taken place in your life that have come through chain reactions—a series of stages or events that precipitated them. Did you recognize God's involvement? Discuss the moments in your life when you were changed for the better while walking through a season of brokenness.

Coaching for Success

The way we view our difficult moments and what we focus on will determine how effective we are at moving forward into our destiny. Here are several keys to maintaining the proper perspective and focus as we travel these journeys.

1. Defend your hope! Hope is critical to the equation of healing and restoration. And it is the foundation of our faith. Hebrews 11:1 says: "Faith is the substance of things hoped for." Hope is the key to enduring the difficult moments and moving on. Hope helps us focus on the big picture of God for our life and on his greater purpose.

2. Release the pain of the immediate situation and embrace the idea that there is something better for you ahead. Seize the opportunity that a season of brokenness affords. Often in the process of pain we experience the greatest link to our potential, and to change!

3. Learn to pray daily about your purpose and God's plan for your life. Invite God to help and be involved with all that concerns you.

4. Write your prayers and journal your thoughts regarding your dreams and goals and evaluate your progress, including moments that you know that God is at work in your life.

We've all had moments when we knew that God was at work in our lives. They were obvious moments filled with undeniable divine intervention. But more often, God's activities and involvements in our lives are subtle and may even seem disguised. Often it's only later that we realize that he was at work at all. If he meticulously planned the birth of the church at Pentecost from the foundation of the world, then he clearly has the capacity to plan a destiny for us all. But knowing that destiny requires that we believe.

Faith is the key to endurance, patience and success. Begin today to stand in faith and walk forward by faith. Trust God to do what's right concerning your future. Invite him in prayer to lead you and guide your life, especially through the seasons of brokenness!

Prayer of Reflection

Lord, help me remember that in moments of crisis and trauma you have the greatest opportunity to transform me into my greatest purpose. I believe that often your highest glory can be revealed in my lowest moments. Therefore, grant me the courage and patience to allow your Spirit to work your plan in me even when I don't understand and even when I am experiencing the pain of difficult circumstances. In Jesus' name, Amen.

Chapter Four

THE VIOLENCE OF CHANGE

Key text: Matthew 11:12: "And from the days of John the Baptist until now the kingdom of heaven suffers violence, and the violent take it by force."

Several years ago I heard a prominent minister speak at a conference in Atlanta on the subject "Leadership in Changing Seasons." I was captivated as he went through a series of biblical stories that demonstrated the necessity and power of leadership in changing environments. Even today, almost fifteen years later, I still remember virtually every point that he shared. His basic background story was of young King Josiah, who came to power in Israel in a time of great spiritual darkness. Hilkiah, a righteous high priest, rediscovered the Book of the Law (probably Deuteronomy) in the House of the Lord. Can you imagine that the House of the Lord in Jerusalem had been filled with so many things of the world that the Word of

> Can you imagine that the House of the Lord in Jerusalem had been filled with so many things of the world that the Word of God had actually been lost?

God had actually been lost? There is a sermon in that all by itself! When

Hilkiah discovered the Book, he immediately took it to young King Josiah, who had the book read and realized that much of the calamity going on in his nation was a result of the people turning away from worshipping the true God to worshipping idols. As a result, the young king launched a season of reform and revival that literally transformed the entire nation.

The underscored idea of the minister's message and use of Josiah to illustrate was one of change. Change is nothing new. It's been around since the beginning of time. Many of us have been through change, traumatic change. Most of us define our lives by the changes that have occurred. All it takes is a casual wandering through the family photo album to realize that all of our lives are pictures and stories of change and process: when the new baby came, the first steps that were taken by that baby as a toddler, perhaps the first day of school, or graduation, maybe a wedding. All of these are pictures of change. And what about the clothes? When I look at those albums I can't believe I wore some of that stuff! I'll bet you'll be reminded that styles have changed as well, or maybe you'll be amazed at how they have made a cycle and what you're wearing today looks a little like something you used to wear years ago. In these books are the records of our times, and the changes we have experienced during those periods of time.

Many of these changes were uncomfortable. But change often is. And I have to be honest: it seems that many of the changes in my life have been initiated by God. I go so far as to think, "I wish God would get it right and leave it alone." The reason change is often described as traumatic is because, in a way, change is violent. There is a violence involved in leaving the comfort zones of our lives and entering something new. For the most part it is violence to our emotions, to our

> There is a violence involved in leaving the comfort zones of our lives and entering something new. For the most part it is violence to our emotions, to our ways of thinking, and to our routines.

ways of thinking, and to our routines.

Being a traveling minister and a coach to Christian leaders for years, for me to speak about change is a common subject. Frequently I tell people that crisis is found on the curve of change, but that the curve only becomes a dead end if you fail to make the turn. Change has always been traumatic and filled with crisis.

This idea can be underscored by part of a letter cited in the book, *The Second Reformation: Reshaping the Church for the 21st Century*. It is a letter sent to President Andrew Jackson in 1829 from Martin Van Buren. Van Buren, then governor of New York, sees the coming of the railroad as a threat to the economic and social well-being of his constituents and, therefore, was motivated to write the President in an attempt to stop the process of change—unwelcome change, he believed—that the railroad would bring.

January 31, 1829
Martin Van Buren
Governor of New York

To President Jackson:

The canal system of this country is being threatened by a new form of transportation known as "railroads." The federal government must preserve the canals for the following reasons:

One. If canal boats are supplanted by "railroads," serious unemployment will result. Captains, cooks, drivers, hostellers, repairmen and dock tenders will be left without means of livelihood, not to mention the numerous farmers now employed in growing hay for the horses.

Two. Boat builders would suffer and towline, whip and harness makers would be left destitute.

Three. Canal boats are absolutely essential to the defense of the United States. In the event of the expected trouble with England, the Erie Canal would be the only means by which we could ever move the supplies so vital to waging modern war.

As you may well know, Mr. President, "railroad" carriages are pulled at the enormous speed of fifteen miles an hour by "engines" which, in addition to endangering life and limb of passengers, roar and snort their way through the countryside, setting fire to crops, scaring livestock and frightening women and children. The Almighty surely never intended that people should travel at such breakneck speed.[8]

Of course, we know what happened. The railroads did come and with them, no doubt, many of Van Buren's concerns were realized. But of course, railroads advanced the country, and immeasurably so, far more than canals could do. Though resisted, the change that was coming could not be stopped.

There is a favorite story I love to tell about the way many of us view change. It's the story of a hound dog that is sitting under a porch in a cool spot on a hot day. The hound dog is howling at the top of his lungs. As a man passed by, the owner of the dog was out front,

> We know something is up; we have become very uncomfortable with the status quo, but the potential trauma we perceive in change causes us to stay in our comfort zones.

and the man asked the owner what was wrong with the dog. "He's sittin' on a thorn", the owner said. "Why don't he move?" asked the man. The owner replied, "It's easier to howl." And that sums up, for most of us, how we view change. We know something is up; we have become very uncomfortable with the status quo, but the potential trauma we perceive in change causes us to stay in our comfort zones. And most of the time we wind up simply howling because of our discomfort.

While coaching people over the years through numerous transitions,

I've used the principles below for effective life transition.

The Ten Commandments of Change

1. Be respectful of things accomplished in the past and to those who accomplished them.

2. Separate ideas from people; ideas are expendable, people are not.

3. Remember that anything that is for the cause of Christ and the kingdom of God is for us.

4. Value criticism and use its potential; allow it to make you better.

5. Count the cost. Do a thorough analysis of the potential impact of the change you are about to make.

6. Honor your present commitments.

7. Maintain an optimistic attitude.

8. Practice expanding your imagination.

9. Communicate, communicate, communicate. Remember to coach the people you are working with through change.

10. If at first you don't succeed, then try and try again.

Change Your Climate

When we think about change, it's important to understand that for a leader change is a way of life. I work with leaders of every shape and size and literally all types of backgrounds every day, but one thing that I have identified that is common among them is the fact that they are each, in some way and to some degree, agents of change. Leadership by its very nature is about change. It is about moving from one position or place to another. To be a leader we must have followers either directly or indirectly—and this implies change. Often we get leadership and management confused. But they are really not the same. *Leadership is about change, progress, and movement, while management is about maintenance of systems, preservation, and sustaining the status quo.* While we absolutely need both types of positions in our society, they are completely different concepts.

In leadership, creating the right environment is the critical first step to successful accomplishment. You might say there is a climate for success. But one of the great challenges faced by leaders is how to create the right environment for the vision they want to accomplish. Often it requires altering an existing climate in a profound, or at least significant, way.

Recently a friend of our ministry, Bishop Tudor Bismark, during a message made reference to the concept of climate in a spiritual context. It got my attention so I thought I would do a little research and see if there were additional spiritual applications and principles to be learned from the natural science of climatology.[9]

The word *climate* comes from the Greek word *klima*, which refers to the inclination of the sun. It is defined as the long-term effect of the sun's radiation on the earth's atmospheric layers. The atmosphere is determined in a region by the combination of average temperatures and the amounts of precipitation that a particular region receives. This atmospheric condition, when consistent over time, will have a tremendous effect on the climate. Simply put, sustain a certain atmosphere and you create a particular climate.[10]

Another important fact related to climate: the kind of life that a particular environment can sustain is determined by its climate. A particular climate allows for certain creatures to survive, even thrive, within its environment, while others either adapt, exit, or become extinct. Changing the climate can be traumatic. Ask the dinosaurs.

Now let's make spiritual applications. When attempting to fulfill a vision, we often face resistance because our vision requires the creation of a new climate. Perhaps the existing climate cannot support the vision that we have and, therefore, we must produce change in the climate. ***When resistance comes—and it always does—we can allow it to become our focus and rob us of our clear, forward vision.*** All we can see at that point is the immediate chaos caused by the trauma of change. This almost always leads to a sequence that certainly produces failure. To be effective we must focus on sustaining the atmospheric condition that will eventually alter the entire climate to a suitable environment for accomplishing the vision that

God has given us. Here's another way to put it: don't fight with people! Create an atmosphere and sustain it. People who are not intended by God to be with you will migrate out, and those who are will adapt to the new climate.

John and Jesus: Agents of Change

We can see this reality at work in the Days of Jesus as well. The coming of John the Baptist and the arrival of Jesus produced tremendous change in the religious climate of that day. Much of the reason that both Jesus and his cousin John were rejected and hated by the Pharisees was because of the revolutionary ideas that they shared and the incredible reception they received from the people. They certainly were agents of change in the environment of first-century Israel. This explains many of Jesus' statements that often have been misunderstood, for example:

> *"And from the days of John the Baptist until now the kingdom of heaven suffers violence, and the violent take it by force" (Matthew 11:12).*

I have heard this passage preached from a thousand different angles, but I never realized that the violence that Jesus was speaking of was the violence of change. It's really quite clear when you look at the context. John is in prison awaiting execution, and he sends his remaining disciples to Jesus for a word of confirmation. Jesus speaks with them, encouraging them to report to John the things they had seen and heard, and then dispatches them back to John. Jesus then turns to a crowd filled with all sorts of people, including members of the religious community from Jerusalem, and explains to them that John did not come to do ministry in such a way that would meet with their approval or that would fit into the confines of what was expected in the contemporary religious culture. And neither did Jesus.

John came offering baptism in the Jordan River—this was a form of ritual cleansing previously reserved exclusively for use in the temple precincts and synagogues. Now he was offering it in simple response to the repentance of sins. This upset the religious hierarchy in Jerusalem.

John preached the right message and lived the right way, but because he wouldn't do it *their* way (the familiar way of the religious system), the religious leaders accused him of having a devil. On the other hand, Jesus came eating and drinking with tax collectors and sinners, and the religious accused him of being a glutton and a drunk, saying he did not possess the proper reputation to be a true prophet.

> John did not come to do ministry in such a way that would meet with their approval or that would fit into the confines of what was expected in the contemporary religious culture.

The truth was, however, that neither Jesus nor John cared about what the religious system demanded. Their mission was to build relationship between God and man, not to redeem religion.

So I believe, in context, that the kingdom of heaven that Jesus spoke of as experiencing violence since the coming of the days of John was the religious system that had become corrupt and existed more to maintain control of the people than to establish the people's relationship with God. The "violent [who] take it by force" were John and Jesus, whose ministries and messages had been widely accepted by those in the common culture, and as a result were liberating God's people from the bondage of religious abuse and control that the Pharisees had put upon them.

The pendulum of change was swinging through the arena of the religious status quo like a demolition ball, and its coming brought a sort of violence to the thought patterns and practices that had perpetuated a religious, but godless, system. Again, the ones swinging this pendulum were Jesus and John.

The violence of change is always present on a road to destiny, and our pilgrimage to our own moment of destiny, our own Pentecost, will undoubtedly involve the same. It helps if we understand this reality. Much of the pressure exerted on the disciples, and causing the events that would lead them into the critical mass of the movement, was the extremely traumatic change germinated within the religious arena as a result of the ministries of first John and then Jesus.

The coming of both John and Jesus signaled an acceleration in the race toward the destiny of the church, and with it a violent trauma within the kingdom of heaven on earth. If the destiny of the church is Pentecost and with it a powerful revelation of peace with God and the purpose of the church, we must understand that often peace and rest are preceded by the violence of change.

The same is true with your life and destiny as well. If you are moving, you are changing. Change is necessary, and it is the demand of progress. When working toward your purpose you will naturally encounter resistance. But if you refuse to quit, it will make you stronger. And with every change you survive, you come closer to Pentecost.

Impact Points

1. **John and Jesus were agents of change and arrived in due season according to God's plan.** But the majority of those involved in the mainstream religious system were blinded by the trauma caused by the magnitude of the change that their messages and ministries created. Change is the most unnatural—and yet, at the same time, natural—thing that we do. Change is part of life and the headwaters of your future. It is life's most basic vital sign. As were the Jews and the nation of Israel during Jesus' ministry, we can be locked in "the now" and fail to experience God's "next" until we are willing to

embrace the necessary change.

Matthew 3:11: "I indeed baptize you with water unto repentance, but He who is coming after me is mightier than I, whose sandals I am not worthy to carry. He will baptize you with the Holy Spirit and fire.'"

2. **Change can be traumatic.** In a way, it causes a sort of violence to our personal patterns and comfort zones.

Matthew 11:12: "And from the days of John the Baptist until now the kingdom of heaven suffers violence, and the violent take it by force."

3. **During seasons of change, the more flexible, pliable, and adaptable we are, the greater our success will be going into the future.** Relax! Change will force your faith to a new level, but as your faith goes to a new level, so will your potential.

Psalms 103:2: "Bless the LORD, O my soul, and forget not all His benefits."

For Group Discussion or Self-Reflection

Take a moment and dream. Dream about your future. Imagine what God could use you to accomplish. We must learn to practice living in the future through our imaginations. The imagination is a tremendous resource, but it must be developed to be effective. Write your dreams, record them, and occasionally take them out to evaluate, pray over them, and use them to help maintain your faith focus. Something amazing will happen. Dream!

Coaching for Success

When we dream about the future we become acutely aware that there is a gap that exists between the dream we have had and our current reality. For us to experience our dream becoming a reality, we must narrow the distance between our "now" and our "next" by making a move, making a change. This move or change should not be done arbitrarily or simply be a change for the sake of change, but it should be purposeful. The purpose of a change or move is to close the gap between where we are and where we want to be. We must navigate the gap! Remember, change almost always feels like loss to us, at least at first, so we must have a clear focus on the new reality of our goal and how it will be better than what we are experiencing now.

Closing the gap, like any journey great or small, will require the following:

1. It will take time, so be patient! And the greater the change, the greater the time needed. Every journey ahead begins with a single step forward.

2. It will take a vehicle. In this context, I see the vehicle as a plan. Essentially, a plan is the strategy that connects where I am to where I want to be. This requires a realistic understanding of my location, a vision, accurate information, and a sense of direction. Educate yourself! Study *you* until you have a good grasp of who you are, where you are, and where and who you want to be. Don't live your life by chance! Live on purpose! This will require a plan.

3. It will require fuel (resources). Depending on the size of the gap you're trying to close, you will need the resources to not only initiate the journey but also to sustain movement. This sustained movement will create momentum, and with greater momentum the action will require less energy. Most energy required for change is spent getting started. Don't lose heart. The beginning is the hardest part.

4. It will require commitment, so find a coach. The best way to remain

committed to a plan is to be accountable to someone else who believes in the vision. Develop a relationship with someone who understands change, how to achieve it, and understands where you are trying to go.

Change can be intimidating, but if you follow these simple steps your rate and success of change can be greatly enhanced.

Prayer of Reflection

Lord, change is often difficult for me. As a result, I find myself resisting what you are trying to do in my life. I realize that change is your way of moving me toward my destiny. Please give me the peace to know that you are as much God in my "now" as you will be in my "next," and that I can trust you with my future without reservation.

Chapter Five

THE ROAD TO CAESAREA PHILIPPI

Key Text: Matthew 16:13: "When Jesus came into the region of Caesarea Philippi, He asked His disciples, saying, 'Who do men say that I, the Son of Man, am?'"

I'm a pilgrim, a traveler. Have been all my life. My first major trip was with my parents, who were pastors in rural Arkansas, and it was an amazing world tour that included Europe and Israel and Jordan in the Middle East. We visited the Sistine Chapel in Rome, where I was dazzled by the brilliance of Michelangelo. Then on to Israel where the Scriptures came alive in each site we visited. And finally to Jordan; we even rode horseback into Petra, the famed Jordanian city that is half as old as time. That trip put a spark in my heart to explore. I guess the great revelation that I had on that trip was of the largeness of our world and its diversity in both its geography and its people. Since that time I've traveled much more! I have longed to know what is over the next hill? Who lives there? How do they live? The adventure of exploration and discovery has become a huge part of my life.

And now I've traveled in ministry for more than twenty years. I've had the privilege to see some amazing sights along the way. I've stood on the Great Wall in China and looked over Victoria Falls on the Zambezi in

Zambia. I've stood in awe of the wonder of the Canadian Rocky Mountains and in sadness among the people of the dump in Managua, Nicaragua.

On my journeys I've seen unspeakable beauty and majesty, and unthinkable poverty and brokenness. On the winding roads I've traveled I've seen highs and lows, the best of humanity and the worst—but I must also say that I have been changed along the way. I have learned much about life and the people who have become a part of it as a result of these journeys. But my greatest discovery has been who I am. Or maybe I should say who I've become. Roads leading away, when traveled, will do that for you. You cannot remain who you have always been when you leave where you are and go someplace new. So, in a sense, roads are our passages into our potential and into lands of undiscovered possibilities. I love roads!

> But my greatest discovery has been who I am. Or maybe I should say who I've become. Roads leading away, when traveled, will do that for you.

Several roads are mentioned in the Scriptures. And they are mentioned because of the incredible events that happened on or near them. On a recent visit to Israel our guide, Ronny Simon, a retired Lt. Colonel in the Israeli Defense Forces and a Jewish historian, explained to us that the history of ancient Israel—like the history of all of civilization—is the story of roads and water. On our trip he spent a week teaching us about both during ancient times in Israel. I think I learned more about Israel and the Jewish people on that trip than any Holy Land trip I had ever taken. *His explanations of where the water sources were located and how the roads developed nearby helped put the entire story in perspective and helped clarify both the people and their culture.* It dawned on me that when you study the history of human civilization, our collective life story, it happens almost exclusively on or near roads.

When I think about the roads mentioned in Scripture, several jump out in my mind: among them, the lonely and desperate path that Adam and Eve must have traveled out of Eden following their sin, and the road Abraham traveled from Ur toward his destiny. He left looking for what he thought was a city "whose builder and maker is God" (Hebrews 11:10). He found his destiny in a promise, not a brick and stone city. And then there was the famous road trip of Jacob, who was leaving town because he had cheated his brother not once, but twice. It caused his parents to suggest he relocate, find a wife, and get on with his life. And stay away, at least until his brother cooled off. As he traveled he stopped near the area of what would one day be Jerusalem, camped for the night, and had a dream that would become the defining moment of his life. We can remember when Jacob traveled a dusty road from Palestine to Egypt to escape a devastating famine and wound up discovering that it was God's providence that had led he and his sons there. And this led to the patriarch being reunited with his long lost child, Joseph, that he loved so much and had thought was dead.

What about in the New Testament? The story of the Good Samaritan takes place on the road to Jericho. And then there were a couple of Jesus' disciples who become believers in the resurrection on the famous road to Emmaus. Paul's conversion, his destiny moment, takes place on the road to Damascus in a vision of the Lord Jesus. And his life is radically transformed at that moment on a dusty road. ***It's really amazing, when you think about it, how many of the Bible stories that we all know and love took place on famous roads.***

And you are a traveler on the road of life as well. You are on a journey out of your past and into your future, away from where you are now and toward where you're going to be and who you're going to become. And no doubt you've had your share of experiences as well, some that brought tears and others that brought joy. Experiences that happen on the roadways of life will almost certainly include tears, terrors, and triumph. And so we travel on, celebrating the victories and mourning the defeats. It is the human experience. Roads—and our travels—are part of life!

There is another road that is as important as any I've mentioned. And it is critical to the story of redemption and the pilgrimage that the redemptive purpose of God is making toward its fulfillment at Pentecost. And if the movement is to arrive in Jerusalem for the Feast of Pentecost and its destiny moment, divine providence would demand that it travel through a very unlikely—perhaps *the* most unlikely—place in Israel, maybe even the entire world: the city of Caesarea Philippi. On the road to Caesarea Philippi the redemptive movement would make a hard turn into the unexpected and from here it would begin to move metaphorically downhill and create a momentum that, from this moment on, would be unstoppable. The pressure on the atom of God's plan really began to increase as Jesus led his disciples to this place.

The Road to Caesarea Philippi

Caesarea Philippi was a Roman resort city situated in the foothills of Mount Hermon, the second-highest mountain in the Middle East, rising to about 9,200 feet. The city itself was 1,100 feet in elevation, and together the city and mount created an imposing landmark that could be seen from quite a distance as you traveled toward them. The city was twenty-five miles north of the Lake of Galilee, forty-five miles south of Damascus, so not very far from the international trade routes that converged in Damascus. There was water there, lots of it. From the snowy melts of Mount Hermon the headwaters of the Jordan River began and flowed out into the stream, from a cave in the rocky cliffs, that created a backdrop for the city. It was—and is—a beautiful place.

> From the snowy melts of Mount Hermon the headwaters of the Jordan River began and flowed out into the stream, from a cave in the rocky cliffs, that created a backdrop for the city. It was—and is—a beautiful place.

Consequently, it was filled with all the trappings you would expect from a vacation spot with a cosmopolitan flare. But among the Jews it had a bad reputation. You might say it was the "Vegas" of Palestine. Anything and everything you could imagine in the way of sensuality and immorality was available in Caesarea Philippi. There was plenty of idolatry as well. It was an international city within the borders of Israel that Romans and international travelers would resort to for all the comforts of home, including their Greek gods. All that the pagan world had to offer was showcased there on clear display.

The principle Greek god that was worshiped there was Pan. Pan was the half-goat, half-man creature that was the Greek god of desolate places and carnal desire; it was even associated with terror. Incidentally, it's from this god, Pan, that we get our word *panic*. There was actually a temple built to venerate Pan—and the cult that was associated with him—at the mouth of the cave from which the water flowed. As you would imagine, the Jews hated everything that this city represented. The Jews had a nickname for the temple of Pan and the cave from which the stream flowed. They called it the gates of Hades. The Jews were actually forbidden by rabbinical teaching to even go there.

> The Jews had a nickname for the temple of Pan and the cave from which the stream flowed. They called it the gates of Hades.

It was to this spiritually repugnant and morally corrupt place that Jesus took his disciples to dramatically turn their focus toward their real mission and ultimate destiny. Against the backdrop of all that the world had to offer, and their greatest fears, Jesus would reveal to his disciples what really matters in life. They would discover their authority and ultimate purpose and get their first glimpse into the events that would shortly follow. The road to Caesarea Philippi was the location for a critical turning point on the road to destiny for the redemptive movement. But to understand it fully we have to look at the Jewish environment at the time.

The story takes place during a time of extreme political intrigue and social upheaval that was largely created by the massive impacts of the message and ministries of Jesus and John. A wide range of feelings and emotions among the people were beginning to surround their lives and ministries. And the people's response was reaching a fevered pitch. The common people hated the oppression of the foreign invaders who had imposed their will on the people. And it had largely been the condition of the common people for hundreds of years. They longed for deliverance. Both John and Jesus came into this world with a radical flare that ignited the people with great hope for change.

The Question We All Must Face

John had now taken a major step that could have been interpreted as a step toward revolution. He began criticizing the king, Herod. I mean, it's one thing to preach to the people, but he had then turned his focus to the highest levels of the Jewish government. He was arrested for it—and eventually executed. People must have expected that that would be the moment for a revolution. John's death had created a vacuum of power. He carried so much weight with the people because he was the first prophet to speak God's Word to Israel with any real credibility for more than four hundred years. The corruption of the Jewish temple and even priesthood itself had left them with no confidence in the current religious system. So John's following among the common man was huge. And now he was dead.

Of course, Jesus was the biggest factor of all! John actually had pointed him out as the long-awaited Messiah; Jesus had been performing miracles for more than two years. *He had demonstrated all that the common people had expected the Messiah to do—except form an army. His words were powerful, his actions equally powerful.* People would follow him if he would lead them. Even the power brokers from the religious establishment in Jerusalem came to Jesus in that moment filled with uncertainty after John's death and asked Jesus to perform one more sign to prove his identity. But he refused!

It must have been a shock to His disciples. They were still unclear themselves concerning Jesus' actual mission. They, like most Jews, expected a warring Messiah, a Moses-like figure who would lift the yoke of oppression from the weary neck of the Jewish culture, set up his kingdom in Jerusalem, and drive out the foreign influence of the Greeks and Romans, all while restoring a purified Judaic worship in Jerusalem with an authentic Aaronic priesthood.

They surely wondered: *Perhaps he will use this moment to ascend to power? Maybe John's death would signal the time for action?* Questions and hopes about who Jesus actually was must have been boiling in the hearts and minds of the people. Change was in the air! But what type of change would it be? Would it be revival, a cleansing of foreign influence and interference? Or, did it mean something totally new and different? Was Jesus the long-awaited Messiah? Or just another of the more than forty imposters who claimed to be Messiah and gained a following but in the end had come to nothing?

Jesus and his followers had really turned the Jewish community on its head. The common people were elated, the religious establishment was concerned, and the political leaders were beginning to take notice. And right in the middle of all of this turmoil, Jesus tells his disciples that they're taking a road trip.

So out of their comfort zone of the familiar surroundings of Galilee he led them. The disciples might have said, "Wait! Where are we going?"

Jesus: "You'll see."

The disciples: "But we don't normally go this way. Why Lord?"

Jesus: "Trust me. I want to show you something."

What confusion and conflict they must have felt. Have you ever felt like that? Have you ever felt that following Jesus required more than you were prepared to give? That you must go further than you intended to go? Then you've been there! There, with Jesus on the road to Caesarea Philippi. On this road you must leave your comfort zone and tidy conveniences of everyday ritual to go to a place you have never gone before, to a place that makes no sense to the natural mind, and will test everything you thought you believed.

Jesus no doubt waited until they were within visible range of the city, with its lofty cliffs and demonic temple. He turns to confront his very own followers with two questions. The first, though, was merely a leading question. It really just set up the other. His first question was, "Who do men say that I, the Son of Man, am?" They responded, "Some say John the Baptist, some Elijah, and others Jeremiah or one of the prophets." But you get this feeling that Jesus was not concerned with the political pundits in Jerusalem or what the religious commentators were saying about him. It was really just a question that opened the door to another. And it is the question that we all are brought to Caesarea Philippi to answer.

Jesus asked, "But who do *you* say that I am?" Here is my paraphrase of that question: *Who am I to you?* And this is the question of all questions, for all of us and certainly for the disciples at that moment. There was no progressing beyond this point. Against the vivid

> Jesus knew what was ahead and that only a firm faith in his identity as Messiah would allow them to weather the coming storm and complete the rest of the journey.

paganism, worldly pleasures, and fears of the world we must decide who Jesus is to us!

Peter, who often gets ahead of himself, speaks up. "You are the Christ, the Son of the living God." This time Peter swung for the fence and knocked it out of the park! That is the gateway conclusion; that is the ticket to the next phase of the trip! We must put Jesus in his rightful place. We must settle it once and for all. You are the Christ! Jesus knew what was ahead and that only a firm faith in his identity as Messiah would allow them to weather the coming storm and complete the rest of the journey.

Destiny is God's plan for you. He has a definite purpose and plan for your life. But that journey will always begin in one way or another with a stop at *your* Caesarea Philippi to answer a question that will define everything in your life—and become the lens through which you will view the rest of the trip!

The Keys of the Kingdom

As we have been discussing this journey toward the destiny of the church at Pentecost, we have discovered that it is a trip we are all taking as well. As we look at the story of Jesus and his disciples we see not only their struggles, but also the stories of their struggles, reminding us of our own, and of the fact that the move toward our destiny follows a common pattern. And it has throughout all of history for all the people of God. There is a beginning with a hope and a promise, and then a journey filled with excitement and sorrow. During the trip we discover truth, meaning, and significance as we pursue the moment where we are truly transformed. For them it was as an early version of the Day of Pentecost, and in a way it is for us as well.

Pentecost was the destination for the redemptive movement, but the road to Caesarea Philippi was an important stop on this journey. Jesus' disciples were certainly challenged by their visit there. And it was there that some things were solidified. Peter declared Jesus to be the Messiah, without question! Now Jesus, following that affirmation, would begin to release more of the story to them than they had previously known.

First, he tells them that his church will be built on the strong

> His church will be built on the strong faith and proclamation of his true identity as Messiah and that even Hell itself will not be able to stop it! As he makes this strong statement he almost surely turns to point to the temple of Pan!

faith and proclamation of his true identity as Messiah and that even Hell itself will not be able to stop it! As he makes this strong statement he almost surely turns to point to the temple of Pan! Remember the Jews called the temple of Pan, which was situated against the rocky cliffs of Caesarea Philippi, the gates of Hades. Jesus, by bringing them to this forbidden place, illustrates to them with an amazing clarity that the message of the Gospel and its believers' assembly will be established even in the most difficult places that they—or we—could possibly imagine. Nothing will be able to stop it. And when we understand that they are now just six months from his passion, from Calvary, we see that it was a revelation that they had to grasp to be able to endure what lay ahead.

Then he gives them a promise! It seems to me that the glue that often holds us in the difficult moments of life is a promise. He says that he will give them keys to the kingdom of heaven, and with the keys great authority both on earth and in heaven. Keys are really a universally accepted metaphor for three things: authority, access, and responsibility. When we have keys we understand that to mean that we have certain privileges, certain prerogatives, that others do not have. We can access things and places that others can't! *But with these privileges come expected responsibilities toward the one who gave us the keys.*

Imagine the impact of this teaching by Jesus to his disciples. There in that wicked place that they had been taught to fear and avoid, he essentially tells them that once they have put him in his proper place they will receive authority and access that will release such power in them that they can speak a word and the effect will be known not only in the most difficult place on earth, but that there will be an immediate effect in the realm of the unseen as well! What a word! In light of all the turmoil of Galilee and the expectations of the people, this is the word they have been waiting on! Let's do this thing! This would have been one of the great 'hurrah' moments of Scripture—if it were not for the next thing that Jesus tells them.

"Don't tell anyone that I'm the Christ." And then, it gets worse.

"From that time Jesus began to show to His disciples that He

must go to Jerusalem, and suffer many things from the elders and chief priests and scribes, and be killed, and be raised the third day" (Matthew 16:21).

Their expectation of a conquering Messiah must now be reconciled with a suffering one. The road to destiny is making a sharp turn; this was a tremendous paradigm shift. Peter responded and underscored the magnitude of the shift when he said, "Far be it from You, Lord; this shall not happen to You!" For this rejection of God's will and plan, Jesus rebuked him. Peter had just made this wonderful declaration of Jesus' Messiahship, and for it received a blessing from Jesus— only to turn and run right back into the very way of thinking that Jesus had brought them to this place to change. As a matter of fact, in this story we see three pictures of the man, Peter, who was in the throes of tremendous change and transition. And he was struggling to make sense of it all.

> Their expectation of a conquering Messiah must now be reconciled with a suffering one. The road to destiny is making a sharp turn; this was a tremendous paradigm shift.

The first picture is of "Simon," Peter's family name. This name is a good, blue-collar "everyday sort of fellow" name. But in his revelation of Jesus' identity he is called by Jesus as "Peter," or a Stone. He goes from an everyday guy to the name that he would be know by as an apostle because of the revelation he's had. ***But then when faced with this hard turn in thinking about the Messiah, he tries to stop the plan of God that had just been spoken by Jesus.*** Then Jesus himself calls him the devil!

> *"Get behind Me, Satan! You are an offense to Me, for you are not mindful of the things of God, but the things of men" (Matthew 16:23).*

Imagine Peter going, in a few moments of time, from a normal guy to an apostle to the devil. It would actually be kind of funny to me were it not for the absolute affinity I have with Peter. I must admit there have been moments in my own journey in which I was elevated to "apostle status" in a revelation, only to come tumbling down from that lofty perch because of my misunderstanding of the plan of God and the constant struggle for my will and plan over God's will and plan. As we travel the road to our destiny, we as humans must constantly reconcile our own will to the will of God. Following God's will keeps us on course; following our own will takes us off course and into the wilderness of disappointment and stagnation and, worse, insignificance.

I'll bet you can relate as well. We often have these preconceived ideas about how things are going to work out, only to be taken to a place, a moment outside of our comfort zones, to get a revelation and some correction for our thinking before we can move on. Caesarea Philippi is a place of clarity, a place of definition. And we might not always like the conclusions we draw there, but if we are willing to embrace God's plan, it can become a place of great hope and authority.

Now, this is all well and good. So God's plan for the Messiah is to go to Jerusalem and suffer. That alone is hard enough for the disciples to process, but it gets even worse, much worse, when Jesus makes one more revelation.

> Then Jesus said to His disciples, "If anyone desires to come after Me, let him deny himself, and take up his cross, and follow Me. For whoever desires to save his life will lose it, but whoever loses his life for My sake will find it" (Matthew 16:24, 25).

Jesus now lets his disciples know the high price of destiny. God has a plan for you, a place of transformation and realization, but to get there you have to be willing to lay it all down! He makes it abundantly clear that not only is he to die, but so are we. Yes, he as Messiah is submitted to the plan of God for his life, but our destiny requires nothing less of us than his did of him. We each have a passion to experience and endure, and to do it we need to first and foremost know who Jesus is to us and then we must know who and whose we are. Yes, there is a purpose and a power to fulfill, but we must stay the course and finish our trip! Caesarea Philippi separates the proverbial men from the boys. Are you willing to join, then, on this amazing road to Pentecost? We will see the destiny of Jesus and the church as it arrives at Pentecost, but realize that ours awaits us there as well. And when we arrive we will learn this lesson, one I've heard many times through the years: "There will never be a head fitted for a crown whose hands haven't been fitted to a cross!"

The timeline of our journey is now becoming urgent and accelerated. In Caesarea Philippi, Jesus reveals the passion that awaits him in Jerusalem, and little did the disciples know that it was only six months in the future. It must have been so much to process. They need something to help them put it in perspective, so while visiting northern Israel just six days later Jesus takes Peter, James, and John up to a high mountain and there before their very eyes he is literally changed—he is transfigured. They see him in his glory! Moses and Elijah, the first representing the Law and the second representing the Prophets, appear there and endorse Jesus and his coming passion. There can be no doubt now! Jesus is the Christ, he was born to die, and in doing so he is fulfilling the will of God. Moses and Elijah give witness to that fact. Now we begin the passion phase of the trip.

> In Caesarea Philippi, Jesus reveals the passion that awaits him in Jerusalem, and little did the disciples know that it was only six months in the future. It must have been so much to process.

Impact Points

1. **Jesus took his disciples out of the familiar and safe Galilee to the godlessly depraved city of Caesarea Philippi.** Sometimes your journey toward your destiny will take you out of your comfort zone and into places that you would not have chosen to go.

   John 10:27: "My sheep hear My voice, and I know them, and they follow Me."

2. **Every journey into God's purpose for our lives requires a clear affirmation of who Jesus is to us.** Against the backdrop of all that the world has to offer and our greatest personal fears, we must admit, as Peter did on the road to Caesarea Philippi, that Jesus is the Christ.

   Matthew 16:13, 14: "When Jesus came into the region of Caesarea Philippi, He asked His disciples, saying, 'Who do men say that I, the Son of Man, am?'
   "'Some *say* John the Baptist, some Elijah, and others Jeremiah or one of the prophets.' "He said to them, 'But who do you say that I am?'"

3. **The keys to the kingdom of God and to our future are linked to our faith in Jesus Christ.** Putting him in his rightful place gives life to the faith that you will need as you travel the road ahead.

   Matthew 16:16: "Simon Peter answered and said, 'You are the Christ, the Son of the living God.'"

4. **Often, our journey toward destiny begins with a vision of success, but we soon realize that our journey involves a process filled with passion and pain.** During their visit to Caesarea Philippi, Jesus reshaped the disciples' vision of the journey ahead. They assumed that they would march victoriously into Jerusalem, but Jesus explained that suffering must precede victory.

   Matthew 16:21: "From that time Jesus began to show to His disciples that He must go to Jerusalem, and suffer many things from the elders and chief priests and scribes, and be killed, and be raised the third day."

For Group Discussion or Self-Reflection

As believers we know that the process of conversion involves believing in our hearts and confessing with our mouths that Jesus is Christ, our Savior and Lord. But being converted is much more than simply making a decision. He then says to us, "Follow me." We must make him Lord of our lives by obeying and becoming a follower, a disciple. Being a follower of Christ means that we must, as the word implies, follow him wherever he leads us. Discuss what that has meant to you and in what ways you have followed Jesus. Where has that pilgrimage taken you, through what transitions and transformations?

Coaching for Success:

Making a decision about Jesus' identity is one thing, but all believers must then work through the realities of how that decision must change our normal lives. Below are four simple steps that will aid you in not only becoming a believer in Christ, but a disciple as well.

1. Acknowledge that your natural way of thinking and patterns of life lead you away from God's purpose. We must genuinely realize that a change of thinking and acting is in order.

2. Seek God's ways through a consistent studying of Scripture. Our minds must be transformed through the truth of God's Word. Use a good resource to assist you, like a Bible study guide, book, or workbook.

3. As you study, ask the Holy Spirit to illuminate your mind to the

truth of God's Word.

4. Commit to a lifestyle of prayer and seeking God for guidance in everything you do or say in your life. Invite Jesus to rule in everything.

5. Become part of a faith community. Join a healthy, Bible-believing church or small group so that you have accountability, encouragement, and fellowship.

Prayer of Reflection

Lord, I believe that you are the Savior of the world, that you are the Son of God who came to earth, lived a sinless life, and died a sinner's death, the death that I deserved to die. I believe that you rose again on the third day and ascended to heaven. This I believe and affirm, but I want to be more than a decision for you; I want to follow you, to be your disciple! Help me today to surrender my fears and failures as well as my hopes and dreams to you, to your capable care! My life is not my own—I give it to you. Lead me and I will follow. Show me and I will know the way. Give me courage for the moments that you ask me to go to a place that I would not have chosen, so that there I can know you more. In Jesus' name I pray, Amen.

PART III

Chapter Six

DECISIONS IN THE GARDEN

Key Text: Matthew 26:39: "He went a little farther and fell on His face, and prayed, saying, 'O My Father, if it is possible, let this cup pass from Me; nevertheless, not as I will, but as You will.'"

As we focus on the direct steps that led to the critical mass of the movement and which will ultimately lead to the destiny of the church at Pentecost, let's zero in on the events of the night Jesus was betrayed.

Jesus and his disciples gathered in the upper room in Jerusalem where they would share the Passover meal together. This particular evening would be filled with much emotion and symbolism. On this night two worlds would collide. One, the old and previously in control; the other new and about to take over. One founded on the principle of fear through sin; the other to be established on faith.

This night would include the traditional Passover meal and then be followed by Jesus' farewell address and eventually his betrayal and arrest. But it began with a party. In Eastern cultures, when guests came to a party, a slave in the house would be assigned to wash their feet as they arrived as a sign of welcome and courtesy.

On this night, Jesus himself would assume this humble role of a servant and wash his disciples' feet.

Lessons from Jesus' Final Passover with His Disciples

Passover originally was two spring festivals celebrated in the Jewish month of Abib. One, called the Passover, was celebrated at the twilight of the fourteenth day of the month and was a single day that commemorated the sacrificial lamb slain the night the death angel passed over the homes in Egypt, sparing the firstborn in each home that had the blood of the lamb applied to the doorpost. The other followed the next day and ran for six additional days, making seven in all, and was called the Feast of Unleavened Bread. It had to do with cleansing and removing leaven from the home for seven days, thereby illustrating the need to remove sin from our lives. By New Testament times the two feasts had come to be known as simply the Passover, which was understood to include both.

Together, they were symbolic of deliverance and new beginnings—deliverance through the Lamb that suffered death on their behalf and provided them deliverance from death, which is the result of sin; and new beginnings through the cleansing of old leaven or sin in the house and, thus, starting over again with a clean house absent of corruption or pollution (leaven). This festival was celebrated throughout Jewish history. And the Passover meal was to be viewed each time it was eaten as if it were the Hebrews' last meal in Egypt!

> This festival was celebrated throughout Jewish history. And the Passover meal was to be viewed each time it was eaten as if it were the Hebrews' last meal in Egypt!

In addition, it was believed that the giving of the Law of Moses came fifty days after that first Passover, coinciding with our Pentecost.

By New Testament times the Passover evening meal was held in a home, usually in a courtyard or a room that had been prepared for the event. The lamb was roasted in a clay oven on a pomegranate wood stick, legs unbroken. Inside, the company of people would all be dressed in festive white, the room appointed with cushions for reclining and small tables for serving.

The leader of the meal would sit at the head of the table. Those who participated reclined to show symbolic ease and rest. (It is true that the Passover was eaten in haste in Egypt, and in the desert wanderings. But after entering the Promised Land, the Jews took the meal in these positions of rest to symbolize freedom.) Each had to regard himself or herself as having once actually been in Egyptian bondage and having been delivered. Freedom was the theme.

> At various intervals four cups of wine were consumed. The first two generally represented joy. The third represented redemption and the fourth consummation.

The meal included various symbolic elements, each consumed at specific points throughout the evening: roasted lamb, bitter herbs, unleavened bread, haroset, and a raw vegetable with a tart dip. At various intervals four cups of wine were consumed. The first two generally represented joy. The third represented redemption and the fourth consummation.

Ritual hand washings and prayers were also a part of the evening, as well as singing the Hallel (portions of Psalms 113-118). Then came the focal point of the ceremony: a son would ask his father, "Why is this night different from all other nights?"

The head of the house would then tell the story of the Passover lamb of Egypt.

It was at this point in the evening that Jesus must have said (and this from Matthew 26:26-29), as he took the bread and blessed it, giving it to his disciples: "Take, eat; this is My body." Then he took the cup, and gave thanks, and gave to them, saying, "Drink from it, all of you. For this is My blood of the new covenant, which is shed for many for the remission of sins." Here is my paraphrase of these words: "This is my body. Now you won't look back to the Passover lamb of Egypt, but look to me, the lamb slain before the foundation of the world."

Then Jesus took the cup and blessed it (this was cup three, the cup of redemption) and said, "Everyone of you drink from it, for this is representing my blood of a new covenant which is shed for the remission of sins."

All this fulfilled the prophecy of Jeremiah in chapter 31:31-33:

> "Behold, the days are coming, says the LORD, when I will make a new covenant with the house of Israel and with the house of Judah—Not according to the covenant that I made with their fathers in the day that I took them by the hand to lead them out of the land of Egypt, My covenant which they broke, though I was a husband to them, says the LORD. But this [is] the covenant that I will make with the house of Israel after those days, says the LORD: I will put My law in their minds, and write it on their hearts; and I will be their God, and they shall be My people."

Then came cup four, the cup of consummation. But Jesus refused to drink this cup until he and his disciples could drink it together during the marriage supper of the Lamb—when all the saints would partake of it in the heavenly kingdom (see Revelation 19:7-9).

Jesus' farewell address would center on the coming of the promise of the Father, which he said would take place shortly after his departure from earth.

> The apostle John was so moved by the events and teaching of the last supper that he devotes no less than five chapters—almost one fourth of his Gospel—to record this one night for posterity.

The apostle John was so moved by the events and teaching of the last supper that he devotes no less than five chapters—almost one fourth of his Gospel—to record this one night for posterity. In his mind, as he looked back through the years, he must have viewed that night, that Passover, as a watershed moment in the Christian movement and all of redemptive history. For it would prove to simultaneously be the last and the first—the last celebration of the old with its commemoration of Israel's exodus from natural bondage in Egypt; and the first of the new, which would commemorate a spiritual exodus from the bondage to sin for all mankind. The first had been presided over by Moses, the giver of the Law; the last presided over by Christ, the giver of true, and eternal, life. How fitting that during his last evening with them on earth Jesus would put to rest the old religious economy of works and righteousness with a celebration in its honor called Passover, and at the same time establish a new system, a new covenant of redemption by grace.[11]

In the Garden: The Ultimate Decision

After the supper Jesus and his disciples left the upper room and walked to the familiar Garden of Gethsemane. For them, Gethsemane was a place of refuge far removed from the turmoil of the temple precincts and busy markets of Jerusalem. It was a favorite place to hang out while they were in Jerusalem. From the language of John's gospel it appears to have been a walled garden on the opposite side of Jerusalem, above the Kidron Valley and on the slopes of the Mount of Olives.

On this normally festive night Jesus takes his disciples out to this quiet garden for the evening to rest. But this evening would not be a time of rest for Jesus. He was feeling the force of the weight of all of mankind's sin as it pressured the redemption movement toward its critical mass.

Gethsemane means "oil press," and on this night it lived up to its name. It is hard to imagine the incredible pressure Jesus experienced there. *It was a mental and emotional crushing previously unknown to any man, and certainly one that would never be experienced again.* All that the law of God required, and the satisfaction that it demanded, was placed upon him that night. Every lamb sacrificed throughout history, every scapegoat, every high priest who had ever entered the Holy of Holies to apply the blood to the Mercy Seat, all that were involved in the sacrificial system of the Old Testament—each and every one was gathered in the garden that night to observe. For they all had foreshadowing roles; each bore witness that this day would come, and with it the decision that would be made once and for all by a man, the second Adam, who was God in the flesh.

The decision was whether to surrender to the will of God or to his own will, to honor God's plan or to try to accomplish his mission some other, more comfortable way. The first required sacrifice, the second human ingenuity. This time they could not work in unison. It had to be one or the other. It is a decision every Christian, every true believer, must face at one time or another.

> The decision was whether to surrender to the will of God or to his own will, to honor God's plan or to try to accomplish his mission some other, more comfortable way.

Would Jesus change his mind? How would the fact that he was fully man, as well as God, affect his decision? Would wearing a robe of flesh alter his divine plan? What a decision. The thing is that the mission, the destiny he came to fulfill, left no flexibility in his decision. If man was to be redeemed, there was no alternative. Righteousness made a demand that only his love could satisfy. His choice was clear. He was born for this moment.

His cousin John the Baptist had known it as well as Jesus. Even with their arrivals as violent warriors who came to take the kingdom by force, each knew that this moment would come. For Jesus it would be a moment so violent that the warrior would weep and bleed without a blow being struck. It was a moment when the Warrior-Shepherd would become a lamb. By a simple decision, the point of no return was passed.

We all understand, to some degree, that the environment of this time was filled with political intrigue, both in the religious sector as well as the governmental one. Jesus was about to experience the fury of both.

But neither would compare to the brutality of God's judgment on sin and the burden of the separation, humiliation, and shame that must have been in that bitter cup that Jesus drank that night. Redemption would demand that he drink it all, even though he did not deserve to do so. Indeed, he had to do so willingly if humanity stood any chance of forgiveness and reconciliation with a Holy God.

Obviously, the decision to go ahead must have been the kind of decision that could make you sweat blood, one so unfair as to make your heart break from within. And the time had come that it must be made. It was a moment of decision that would alter the course of history, both before and after. This would begin the final countdown to his destiny—to all of our destinies. It was the critical mass of the redemptive movement and of all history, and the critical mass that would release the fission of the church in just more than fifty days.

It is the moment of decision that would take place in the Garden of Gethsemane that night that would be the place and time where Jesus the man would truly own the reality of his divinity and potential as Messiah. The proof of his mission and divinity was not in the spectacular miracles he performed. It was not in the walking on water or controlling the wind and waves. It wasn't his obvious authority to cast out demons. *Instead, he owns his identity and divinity in a moment of decision where, once and for all, it became clear to him that by drinking that horrible cup he could release all mankind from its chains to sin and death. And he was willing to do so. That is divine.*

In the garden is where the real battle was won. It is as if the forces of good and evil met in vehement conflict that night with everything on the line, Christ's destiny and ours—every man's destiny was up for grabs in a winner-take-all, fight-to-the-death match. By comparison, every encounter between good and evil that preceded this moment in history was simply a skirmish, a preliminary to the main event. David and Goliath, Abraham's test with his son Isaac, Daniel in the lion's den, Elijah against the prophets of Baal—each representing very important battles in this conflict and intensifying pressure on the atom of God's people. But, at the same time, each were simply warmups compared to the engagement that took place in the garden that night.

The great spiritual victory of Christ's resurrection could never have taken place were it not for the decision Jesus made in the garden. Truly, it was a defining moment in the life and mission of our Lord. His destiny was planned before he came. He was to come and live a sinless life, die an atoning death, and be raised again, redeeming man from the fall and the curse of sin and death. On one level, we might say that it sounds simple, right? Every destiny, once accomplished, can seem simple to those looking back on it. But I suggest that every great destiny, while it may be realized in moments of action, is conceived in a moment of decision. While the price of Christ's destiny would be transacted on Calvary, its payment would be appropriated in Gethsemane when Christ said, " . . . not My will, but Yours, be done" (Luke 22:42).

Every journey toward destiny begins in a moment of decision. Decisions dot the landscapes of all of our lives. They are sometimes very difficult and sometimes quite easy. Even so, they are there. We learn to make them at the earliest moments of our lives and continue to learn as we go.

Decisions: The Price of Destiny

Many of the greatest lessons I've learned in life come from children's stories and cartoons. I'll never forget one particular day watching the story of *Alice in Wonderland* with my daughter, Jordan. During the story, Alice comes to the fork in the road, and the hare is sitting there. She asks the question, "Which way do I go?" And he responds, "Where are you going?" She says, "I don't know." And he says—and this is my paraphrase: "Either road will take you there." I realized at that moment that the route you travel toward your destiny is of no consequence if you don't know where you are going. The road you travel is only relevant when you have a clear destination in mind. And if you know where you are going, the decisions you make become all the more critical.

These decisions will often be the ones that have tremendous impact, not only in our lives, but in the lives of others as well. They are decisions that have so much to do with who we are, what we become, and what impact we have on others along the way. It was just this sort of decision that Jesus made that fateful night in the Garden of Gethsemane.

> I realized at that moment that the route you travel toward your destiny is of no consequence if you don't know where you are going.

Decisions are the price of our destiny and of our progress. We all constantly make decisions—where we live, who we marry, and how we spend our money are among the myriad of choices we make that affect our lives and the lives of those around us. The greatest, most catalytic moments of your life are the ones in which decisions are made. But I'm also speaking of decisions that are much more fundamental than those of where we are going to live or what kind of car we drive. They are the kind that have to do with our mission and purpose, how our attitudes are developed, things like forgiveness, and whether to walk in fear or faith. These decisions become the cornerstones of the life that we construct.

Almost every arena of life can reinforce the power and importance of decisions. *Business leaders, athletic stars, and political leaders, if asked, would affirm that in most cases the difference between success and failure, between winning and losing, is not made in the moments of action, but rather in the moments of decision that lay quietly behind them.*

When Jesus said, "Not My will, but Yours, be done," the victory was won. We all must come to that garden of decision and settle our destinies. Win or lose, succeed or fail, it is our decision. But this brings us to the part we can never anticipate. We make the most important decision of our lives and what happens next? Everything is going to be all right now, right? Have you ever felt the disappointment associated with doing the right thing when that right decision, as it turns out, costs you everything?

Jesus went to the garden that night and was faced with the decision of all decisions. He needed someone to pray with and for him—a friend who would sense his need and watch with him. Why could his closest friends not discern the great pressure he was under? Instead of sleeping away the night of his greatest trauma, they should have been watching, more in tune. They should have been helping to carry this load.

> You look for some support, a word, a smile, someone who understands. Instead you are alone with your situation, your struggle.

Ever been there? Faced with the greatest decision of your life? You look for some support, a word, a smile, someone who understands. Instead you are alone with your situation, your struggle. For Jesus, as if having no support in that difficult moment was not enough, it only got worse when the guards came to take him.

And it wasn't just the fact that soldiers and guards came to arrest him like a common criminal—they were led by one of his friends. And Jesus was identified in that midnight hour by a kiss, not an accusation. It only takes a moment to realize that not only has he been without support, but also betrayed by one of his own and abandoned by the rest.

How do you get over that? Many do not. I know people who never get past their garden experience. It is as if they get locked in a time warp and can't get past the pain of the disappointments they have experienced. The abandonment or betrayal of their friends in a moment of crisis has in some way locked them in. You can visit with them years later and find they are still talking about someone who let them down years before. If we're not careful we may still be standing in the garden when we should be at Pentecost. When we should be receiving the power of our destiny, we may be harboring the unforgiveness of the garden. Instead of rejoicing in the freshness of the wind of the Holy Spirit, we may still smell the stale flowers of bitterness and resentment that are products of some painful garden experience.

Yes, my friend, you do have a destiny. God does have a plan for your life and ministry, but don't be discouraged or lose focus when it includes a garden of decision, even if it is a decision that just might cost you everything. Make it and move on. You see, the garden is a stop we all must make on the road to our destiny, but it—the garden—is not your destiny. So don't stay. Go there. Do what you must, and let others do what they will. But refuse to stay too long. Your destiny is not the garden of decision, nor the betrayal we have all experienced there. No, it is just ahead at Pentecost.

Impact Points

1. **Every journey toward destiny begins in a moment of decision.** These decisions are the price of passage into your future. They are the building blocks of the life and destiny that you construct.

   Joel 3:14: "Multitudes, multitudes in the valley of decision! For the day of the LORD is near in the valley of decision."

2. **Making right decisions can have a high price tag attached.** But it is never the wrong time to do the right thing. Right decisions create gravity in our lives.

   John 12:32: "And I, if I am lifted up from the earth, will draw all peoples to Myself."

3. **Making decisions based on your deep convictions allows you to live for a greater purpose.** These decisions add significance to your life.

   James 5:11: "Indeed we count them blessed who endure. You have heard of the perseverance of Job and seen the end *intended by* the Lord—that the Lord is very compassionate and merciful."

4. **Surrendering to God's will often takes the struggle out of the**

decision-making process and releases God's potential into your situation.

James 4:10: "Humble yourselves in the sight of the Lord, and He will lift you up."

For Group Discussion or Self-Reflection

Jesus wrestled with the decision in the garden under so much stress that his sweat became as great drops of blood. Have you ever felt that kind of pressure in a decision? Probably not. But perhaps at some level you can imagine it.

1. What has been the biggest decision of your life to this point, and why?
2. Jesus made the decision in the garden experience to drink the cup of God's wrath against sin. What decision(s) have you made that you felt were right and important, but that were made at some degree of personal sacrifice?

Coaching for Success

As with Jesus in the garden, we too must make difficult decisions. They become the defining moments of our lives. These garden experiences can leave us feeling abandoned, even betrayed. But we must know that the cause that drove us to that particular difficult decision is really a gift that will allow us to live for something greater than ourselves. A life of service and personal sacrifice is the key to living a life of significance.

I'm sure there have been moments in your life when, faced with a big decision, you wished for someone who could help you decide which way to go on the matter. Here are a few keys to navigating important decisions in your life:

1. Do your homework. Gather accurate information and make sure you study it carefully before you draw a conclusion regarding a plan of action. Information is the best foundation for making a good decision.

2. Tune into your internal moral compass. What is the right thing to do? I've always believed that doing the right things over time will cause the right people and right things to be drawn into your life, and into your future, and cause the wrong people and wrong things to leave your life.

3. Seek God's will in the matter and commit to follow it. For us, like Jesus in the garden, the answer to the challenge we face is usually found in whose will we choose to make the priority—God's or our own.

Prayer of Reflection

Lord, it seems that my life is filled with difficult decisions, some with long-lasting, far-reaching consequences. And when facing those kinds of decisions I tend to freeze in fear or feel a sense of dread, even try to micromanage the problem. But Lord, I believe that you are in control of my life and have a destiny for me. Help me to strengthen my faith, courage, and resolve to do the right thing, to do your will. And as I do, I believe that by your grace I will be able to face the challenges of the difficult decisions of life with peace and confidence, knowing that my suffering and sacrifice will result in serving others.

Chapter Seven

THE HOUSE OF CAIAPHAS

Key Text: Matthew 26:57: "And those who had laid hold of Jesus led Him away to Caiaphas the high priest, where the scribes and the elders were assembled."

The Accusation of the Religious

Have you ever been to the house of Caiaphas? I have. I'll bet you have too. If you have ever known the suspicion—or worse, maybe even the rejection—of the very ones who should have been on your side, you have; you've been there. I guess there is no way to get around it, not if you're committed to doing something great for God.

I've been there a few times, once for real. At least that is what the guide said during one of our trips to the Holy Land. We were in Jerusalem and stopped to visit a site that our guide identified as the probable ruins of the palace of Caiaphas, the high priest who interrogated and convened a kangaroo court to try Jesus the night he was betrayed. We saw the dungeon that had no entrance or exit, just a

> We saw the dungeon that had no entrance or exit, just a hole that had been hewn through the rock for a prisoner to be let down by a rope. It was a dreadful place.

hole that had been hewn through the rock for a prisoner to be let down by a rope. It was a dreadful place, even then, after all that time.

As I wandered around and explored the area, I got lost for a moment in my own thoughts about that place and the events that had very possibly occurred at this very site so many centuries before. I guess the emotion that I felt the most was sadness. Sadness because of the way they treated Jesus; sadness for the misunderstandings of the Jews that caused them to miss the greatest opportunity of their lifetimes. Sadness for the ones through history who, like Caiaphas, came face to face with their destiny and took the wrong side, held the wrong position, made the wrong decision. For everyone who has known the pain of rejection, the discouragement of being dismissed as nothing by those who should be celebrating your presence, this story is for you. Jesus knew exactly how that felt.

The night he was arrested and taken to the house of Caiaphas must have been one of the great disappointments of his life. While it certainly did not catch him by surprise, for Israel was notorious for rejecting those who were sent to them by God, it was still, without any doubt, a somber moment of sad confirmation. This moment had been anticipated prophetically and Jesus was all too aware of its approach. As he was led there, I wonder if his proclamation of just a few days prior was on his mind. I could not help but think of his weeping over Jerusalem and longing for a different response from the people. He clearly knew what to expect when he said:

> "O Jerusalem, Jerusalem, the one who kills the prophets and stones those who are sent to her! How often I wanted to gather your children together, as a hen gathers her chicks under her wings, but you were not willing! See! Your house is left to you desolate" (Matthew 23:37, 38).

When you think of the prophets who predicted his coming and the sincere believers who longed for the consolation of Israel, one would think that his coming and their day of visitation would not have been

> They sang songs about it, taught about it, and told stories about what it would be like. They longed for his coming. So why did they miss it when it was right before their eyes?

missed. For generations, the Jews had anticipated the coming of the Messiah. They sang songs about it, taught about it, and told stories about what it would be like. They longed for his coming. So why did they miss it when it was right before their eyes?

Political Parties of First Century Israel

The Essenes: Strict fundamentalist sect of Judaism. Practiced communal lifestyles, for the most part. They were very eschatological and scholarly. Practiced ritual baptism and a communal dinner called the messianic banquet. Best known for the Dead Sea Scrolls found at Qumran, one of their principle communities. It is believed that John the Baptist had roots in this group.

The Zealots: Committed nationalists who resisted taxation and foreign domination and influence. They were generally militant in motivation and tended toward revolt. Simon the Zealot came out of this group to be one of Jesus' disciples.

The Pharisees: The very name means to separate. Considered doctors of the law while the Scribes were laymen. The Pharisees were ardent adherents to rabbinical tradition and were legalistic and spiritual in theology. They believed in the resurrection and the ministry of angels. Had a general disdain for the priesthood due to its corruption.

The Herodians: Secular and supporters of the status quo. Supported the integration of the Greco-Roman culture into mainstream Jewish culture. Joined forces with others in the conspiracy to kill Jesus.

The Sadducees: They were generally the upper class aristocracy who worked closely with the Romans to ensure order and economic stability. Controlled the high priest's office in the days of Jesus and the apostles.

They denied the sovereignty of God and the resurrection of the dead. They were largely in control in the urban and commerce centers.

Ideas of how and when he would arrive were many and diverse. Jewish families were so anxious for him to come that they would normally set an extra place setting at their tables in case the Messiah would unexpectedly show up at mealtime. A seat was also reserved at every synagogue for the Messiah for the same reason. That is what almost got Jesus stoned in Nazareth when, after reading the passage from the prophet Isaiah, he sat down in that special seat and said:

"Today this Scripture is fulfilled in your hearing" (Luke 4:21).

Old Testament prophecies were replete with the hope of his coming. These texts were prominent in the minds of the Jews. How could they not see and realize he was among them? Religious blindness—plain, simple religious blindness.

The sad truth is that often the disease that plagues our vision of God's purposes and our ability to interpret his truth is the blindness of religion. Religion that is not built upon relationship will impair your ability to see and hear the Lord in your day of visitation. Religion alone leaves us with toxic ideas about God and the things of God. It causes us to presuppose certain things about God that may not be accurate and to assume an inflexible posture that is very limiting to our vision and potential. Often self-righteousness and bitterness are the final outcomes of religion without relationship with God.

> Often self-righteousness and bitterness are the final outcomes of religion without relationship with God.

To most Jews in the first century, the Messiah represented something more political than spiritual. Most anticipated a Messiah who would be a great warrior, or who would liberate them from the hand of Roman oppression as Moses had rescued them from Egypt. They expected a Messiah who would set up an earthly kingdom in Palestine with Jerusalem as its capital, and drive out the western invaders, namely the Greeks and Romans. The tragedies of their own experiences had blurred their religious insight and produced a religious mentality with a singular focus on survival and continuation. It was one that is built upon a "me, myself, and I" attitude, which is anti-God and anti-Christ.

This condition was not exclusive to the first century. Many religious institutions are in this same condition today. If you're not like them—if you don't hold the same values and views that they do—then you represent something to be resisted, or at least isolated. I'm not writing of the necessity of sharing a common core of beliefs. We all know that is needed. What I'm referring to is a lack of open-mindedness to the fact that God not only works in our little boxes—and he will do that—but that he very much works outside of them as well. Since so much of this kind of religion is about control, the idea of God doing something that we never would believe he would do, and maybe through someone that we never thought he would use, can frighten us. It can cause us to react in ways that we would not normally react.

Preventing Religious Blindness

Israel missed the identity of the Messiah because of its preconceived religious ideas of who he would be, what he would do, and where he would come from. Basically, the Jewish leaders could not see the truth because they were blinded by their expectations that were based on misunderstanding and misinterpretation of Scripture. If we are not careful we can be affected by the same narrow-mindedness that prevented them from seeing Jesus for who and what he was.

We also have to learn to think outside our situations, our comfortable boxes. Here are several suggestions for doing so:

• Practice using your imagination to think creatively. It is a gift from God and one of the greatest demonstrations of divinity deposited in man. Using your imagination allows you to change your perspective without making a commitment to change your situation. It allows you the opportunity to contemplate other ideas, perspectives, and possibilities in a safe, nonthreatening environment.

• Guard your hope. Hope: This is an attitude of optimism, as well as possibility, and is the garden of potential. Faith will not work if hope is absent (Hebrews 11:1).

• Educate yourself. This requires you to process new information from sources that are outside your frame of reference. Many solutions to your limitations and problematic situations await your discovery in the world of information that education will introduce to you. Albert Einstein said, "The significant problems we face cannot be solved at the same level of thinking we were at when we created them."[12]

• Make right relationships a priority. First seek a proper relationship with God. This will give you the spiritual intuitiveness to hear the voice of the Lord and respond accordingly. Spiritual insensitivity was a primary cause of Israel's lack of awareness of the coming of Christ. Then develop right relationships with others. Relationship is the key to accomplishing anything requiring more than one to achieve.

If you are going to realize your destiny, you will no doubt experience the hostility of religious people whose efforts to maintain their own security and identity will hold you out of your destiny—if you allow it. They, without even knowing it, can lock you into the same prisons of nonprogressiveness that imprison them.

One would hope that after having made the right decision in the garden moments of your life that you would be excused from having to visit the house of the religious. But it just doesn't work that way. This stop awaits all who will not be detoured from or denied their dreams of doing something great for God.

For Jesus, the situation was much the same. The concept of Messiah as Jesus presented himself must have been a challenging one for the Jews to embrace. The idea of a suffering Messiah who would redeem mankind from its greatest oppression, sin, and its resulting alienation from God was outside of their paradigm. For them, the kingdom of God was Israel, and the idea of a universal Messiah whose kingdom was so vast that only the spirit realm could contain it was a completely foreign one.

Jesus for three years had taught that his kingdom was not of this world, but rather was in them—that the purpose of the Messiah was to establish a renewed relationship between God and man. And that, by doing so, he would extend the covenant blessings of Abraham to all who believe—not just the Jews, but to the Gentiles as well. This was an idea that they as a whole could not understand, particularly the professional clergy. They had become comfortable with the Roman occupation. It had even become profitable for them.

An Ironic Encounter

No priest profited from the political and religious bondage of the people more than the high priest and his family. It was they who felt the real threat from Jesus and his teachings. As surely as Jesus had turned their tables of merchandise upside down at his entrance into the holy temple a few days before, they also feared that their entire world and positions were in jeopardy of being turned upside down. And they were.

This fear is what led to the secret arrest of Jesus. Facilitated by his betrayer, Judas, he was arrested and taken from Gethsemane to the house of Annas, and then to the palace of Caiaphas. Caiaphas was the current high priest, and thus, head of the Sanhedrin, the Jewish ruling body.

When Jesus was taken to Caiaphas, two high priests met; both were on trial. It was an extraordinary encounter that could have been the experience of a lifetime for one—had he realized the true identity of the other.

When Jesus was taken to Caiaphas, two high priests met; both were on trial. It was an extraordinary encounter that could have been the experience of a lifetime for one—had he realized the true identity of the other. Little did Caiaphas know that this encounter would engrave him forever in history's "hall of shame." This moment in time would be one pregnant with opportunity beyond anything he had ever experienced or could have hoped to experience as high priest.

As high priest, once a year he entered the famed Holy of Holies with the blood to be applied to the Mercy Seat, and by doing so represented the entire nation before God. Indeed, he interceded for the people to the very One who now stood before him in disguise. Can you imagine Caiaphas coming face to face with the one person—the Eternal Reality—of which his office and service were but a mere shadow? All that his own office as high priest and service in the temple represented was standing before him, the true and eternal High Priest—hands tied, face bruised, red from abuse—and Caiaphas was the judge. What sad irony.

A Place of Testing

The house of Caiaphas? Yes, I've been there. This is a place where you can get messed up. It is a place of testing. Like the garden in many ways, it is a moment of definition. The devil will try to tell you that you have arrived and that this place of rejection is all that God has planned for you, but he is a liar. If you've not been there yet, chances are you will. But it is just another stop on the road to your destiny. Visit but don't stay. Take the test and pass on your way, for there remains a Pentecost for you if you won't quit. When you are met with a word of accusation instead of a word of encouragement, don't panic. It is part of the process. When you visit the house of Caiaphas you join in good company with almost every great Christian leader in history, the greatest of which was a carpenter from an obscure place called Nazareth, one Jesus Christ.

For years many skeptics discounted the Gospel narratives because so little evidence had been discovered that would substantiate the biblical, historical accuracy of the characters and stories. But then in the early 1990s, a group of construction workers, while building a water park near Jerusalem, discovered a burial cave with several ossuaries (burial boxes). Their discovery rocked the religious world. One box had ornate chiseled floral designs befitting a priest of high rank and bore the name *Yehosef bar Qayafa*, or *Joseph, son of Caiaphas*, and included the remains of a man of about sixty, a woman, and four children. It dated from the first century. Scholar Zvi Greenhut, Jerusalem's chief archaeologist, confirmed in a Time magazine article in an August 1992 issue that "it appears that the cave is the final resting place for the Caiaphas family, whose most famous member was the high priest who, according to the Gospels, handed Jesus over to the Romans for crucifixion."[13]

This discovery, the first of its kind, gives solid, confirming evidence of the timeline and existence of one of the lead characters in the proceedings of Jesus' trial. And, as a side note, according to Uwe Siemon-Netto, UPI religious affairs editor, in an article released by United Press International in March 2004, titled "Analysis: Caiaphas—the Real Hypocrite," the woman buried in the tomb of Caiaphas had a coin in her mouth. In the first century pagans would often place a coin in the mouth of a person who had passed away, as payment to Charon, the ferryman taking the dead across the river Styx into Hades, this according to Greek mythology. Siemon-Netto wrote, "This was a sign of unadulterated syncretism, or mixing of religions, indicating that the High Priest's family broke the Second Commandment (Exodus 20:1-5) forbidding idolatry."[14] In other words, Caiaphas could have been a complete phony. He condemned Jesus for blasphemy while he himself may well have been practicing the occult, if these reports are accurate.

Impact Points

1. **If you are committed to doing something great for God, you can expect to be criticized by religious folks** who view your passion for action as a threat to their control.

   Proverbs 25:28: "Whoever has no rule over his own spirit is like a city broken down, without walls."

2. **Beware of the symptoms of religious blindness that can afflict us all.** As with the Jews, who missed the true identity of Jesus because he did not come in the way that they thought he would, or should, we can become blinded by our own preconceived notions of how our destiny should come to pass—and what it should look like when it arrives.

   Isaiah 53:2: "For He shall grow up before Him as a tender plant, And as a root out of dry ground. He has no form or comeliness; And when we see Him, There is no beauty that we should desire Him."

3. **If you are going to realize your destiny, it will often be in spite of people who are blinded by religion.** These people, while trying to maintain their own security, can hold you out of your destiny if you allow it.

   Genesis 37:5: "Now Joseph had a dream, and he told it to his brothers; and they hated him even more."

For Group Discussion or Self-Reflection

Do you need control? How does it express itself? Do you feel critical or hostile toward others or resentful of circumstances that you view as out of your control? List specific examples. Or perhaps you, on the other hand, have felt the hostility of others who viewed you as a threat in the same way those in authority did Jesus. Identify and discuss your experience with controlling attitudes, be they in yourself or others.

Coaching for Success

Religion without relationship causes disappointment and frustration. It leaves the religious with little to hold on to and nothing to achieve except control. Therefore, a person who is committed to a purpose with passion will almost always be viewed as a threat. Focus on the prize and the purpose for which you have been called and move forward with tenacity, while at the same time loving and forgiving those bound with the chains of low expectations.

Commit to allow God to define your destiny. Refuse to become discouraged when your future takes on an appearance that is different from what you had imagined. Live your life for Christ and his purpose, not for the affirmation of man. While standing in love and compassion do not sell out to pressure, burn out during conflict, wash out through fatigue, or fall out with others through offense. Live your convictions and love people.

Prayer of Reflection

Lord, I hate being judged by others when I'm only trying to do what is right, yet I know that this is an experience with which you are well acquainted. Please give me the patience and stamina to keep a right spirit when those who should be helping me seem to be working against me. Lord, I desire to have a gentle spirit and a willingness to endure whatever is necessary for the joy of knowing your purpose and my destiny.

Chapter Eight

THE COURTROOM OF PILATE

Key Text: John 18:37: "Pilate therefore said to Him, 'Are You a king then?' Jesus answered, 'You say *rightly* that I am a king. For this cause I was born, and for this cause I have come into the world, that I should bear witness to the truth. Everyone who is of the truth hears My voice.'"

A Spirit of Control

I'm a big fan of courtroom drama. I suppose it comes from all those episodes of Perry Mason I watched as a kid. It was a regular family event as we watched while Mr. Mason would get to the truth, and with the truth reveal mysterious and often fascinating pieces of a criminal puzzle. And it was always a surprise. Stumped through the entire show, we waited anxiously for the moment of truth. I would sit captivated; I even wanted to be a lawyer for awhile.

And who could not help but be intrigued, in more recent history, by the O.J. Simpson trial in 1995? That trial really reconnected this nation to the drama involved in a public trial of a high profile defendant and opened the floodgates to a now steady stream of courtroom drama to satisfy the appetite of a curious American public.

But the most gripping trial in all of history was not O.J.'s. Nor was it played out before us on the silver screen or small screen. No, this was a trial held long ago in a Roman courtroom, and Truth—absolute Truth and Love—was the defendant. It wasn't a real trial, though. I mean not a legitimate trial where you have the accused, proper legal representation, the presentation of evidence, a jury of the defendant's peers, and so on. No, this was a courtroom and a trial in the purest form. It was right versus wrong, good versus evil, hope versus despair. It was religion and power versus truth and love. But make no mistake about it, it was a trial filled with all the drama, suspense, and emotion that even Hollywood, with its immense creativity and technology, could never have imagined or portrayed. This was not the trial of the century. It was the trial of history, one with universal and cosmic implications. It could be said that God's redeemer being placed on trial was a drama that had been anticipated and expected since the beginning. It would be the trial when the Creator of the universe would stand in judgment by the created and then be sentenced to die for committing the most unthinkable of crimes against society: he loved them enough to tell the truth.

> This was not the trial of the century. It was the trial of history, one with universal and cosmic implications.

Oh yes, truth can be a crime when a lie is the norm. It can be absolutely criminal when it represents the antithesis of society's values. And love of the true kind is as equally reprehensible when only love for one's self is the law of the land. Yes, Jesus must have appeared quite the villain and extremely revolutionary in contrast with the two streams of reality that flowed into the courtroom that day. These two great influences were there to stand in judgment, as they always have when truth and love are on trial. These two spiritual allies are always around, seeking to maintain order, one motivated from one perspective and one from another—one religious, the other political. Their purpose is the same: control.

The figurehead of the proceeding was the newly appointed military governor of Judea, Pontius Pilate. He had only been in power since around the time that John the Baptist had made his initial appearance. He was not such a bad man by contemporary standards. Cruelty and violence were simply tools to maintain order and control. And he used them like a master. He had a job to do, and his performance was being evaluated by the Jews, as well as the political power brokers in Rome. He was a professional man, a career fellow, a man climbing the military ladder toward greatness. He was not religious; he was political. His idea of religion was that of a tool to pacify the people, not to be taken seriously except to the extent that it could be manipulated to suit his ends.

> He was not such a bad man by contemporary standards. Cruelty and violence were simply tools to maintain order and control. And he used them like a master.

When he examined Jesus, he found no fault in him, no grounds to be concerned with or even threatened by this king of a kingdom of love and truth. Pilate realized that Christ's kingdom and philosophy were so far removed from the natural order of life and society as to be no threat at all, and consequently sought to dismiss the charges against him. But he needed his partner in control: religion. He realized he must pacify the religious establishment of Jerusalem if he was to maintain his political influence and power, so he looked for common ground, a place for compromise. Perhaps they could release a killer and then kill love and truth in his place, and by doing so have peace in the kingdom.

Compromise has a strange logic. It is often part of the lexicon of betrayal. It robes itself in nobility and the disguise of the greater good, and parades itself as right, given the situation and circumstance. It is a favorite tool of politicians and diplomats.

If compromise does not work, religion will be ready, stepping in and demanding submission and satisfaction. These two are familiar spirits, seeking the same end from different perspectives, and are really simply disguises for the same spirit.

When Jesus Stood Before Pilate . . .

If you are a leader, you have or will find yourself in this courtroom. If you love Christ and others and follow truth, you will be tempted by one or both of these spirits. You might be charged with crimes against a perverse society, maybe branded a rebel, a seducer of the people, a conspirator against the existing kingdom. Be careful when you color outside the lines, when you march to the beat of a different drummer, because if a spirit of control has its way, that drummer will be playing your death march. But as you march, look down. I'll bet you can't count the footprints in the sand. Many loving truth-seekers have walked this road ahead of you as they turned their backs on what was politically correct and abandoned the confines of religion that is absent of relationship in an attempt to follow their leader, the king of love and truth, Jesus Christ.

> *"If anyone desires to come after Me, let him deny himself, and take up his cross, and follow Me. For whoever desires to save his life will lose it, but whoever loses his life for My sake will find it"* (Matthew 16:24, 25).
>
> — *Jesus Christ*
> *King of love and truth*

Impact Points

1. **If you have more than one person, you have a society, and if you have a society, you have politics.** We in the church talk a lot about

religious spirits, and they are a reality with which we must contend, but we also must deal with political dynamics as well. Jesus did.

Matthew 27:12, 13: "And while He was being accused by the chief priests and elders, He answered nothing. Then Pilate said to Him, 'Do You not hear how many things they testify against You?'"

2. **Compromising with controlling spirits will always be lethal to your vision.** Compromise has a strange logic. It is often part of the lexicon of betrayal. It often robes itself in the disguise of the greater good and parades itself as right, given the situation and circumstance. But it has a purpose: control. You must have the freedom to pursue, develop and experience your vision without the interference of spirits of control.

Matthew 27:24: "When Pilate saw that he could not prevail at all, but rather that a tumult was rising, he took water and washed his hands before the multitude, saying, 'I am innocent of the blood of this just Person. You see to it.'"

For Group Discussion or Self-Reflection

We have all had to deal with politics: on our jobs, among family, and even at church. When people are interacting with one another, the political dynamic will always be present. Most people feel frustrated by it because it pushes us to take sides with some against others. Discuss an experience, or experiences, that you had where you were forced into the uncomfortable game of politics.

Coaching for Success

Jesus' condemnation came through a compact of mutual preservation between the religious and political systems of the day. To safeguard your destiny from the wiles of both, focus on the truth. Truth is the nature of all justice and lasting achievement. And it will be the hinge on which your destiny will swing. Determine that truth is something that you won't compromise. It is the foundation of your future.

Prayer of Reflection

Lord, I understand that often a vision can be destroyed by the force of pressure created by controlling spirits attempting to maintain control. I am aware that your truth is my only refuge. Help me to carefully build my life and destiny on the rock-solid foundation of truth and love. Let me not be shaken by the resistance, even hostility, of others who have their own agendas. But lead me and keep me on your paths as my future is tested by the status quo.

Chapter Nine

CALVARY: THE DEATH OF A DREAM

Key Text: Matthew 27:22: "Pilate said to them, 'What shall I do with Jesus who is called Christ?' They all said to him, 'Let Him be crucified!'"

Never underestimate the power of a dream. A dream can fill a humdrum life with excitement. It can chase away depression and banish despair. A dream can bear the burden of oppression. It is hope with pictures, pictures that are developed in the imagination. They are the vision of what could be and should be, and of what is most important in our lives.

> In a way, we are never more like God than when we dream. It is one of our greatest and most distinctive of human qualities.

When he created us, God gave each of us the capacity to dream. At that moment of creation he designed us with the ability to reason, with free will, and he gave us the ability to imagine as well. It is one way we can make the connection to our divine origin. In a way, we are never more like God than when we dream. It is one of our greatest and most distinctive of human qualities.

Through history, men and women with a dream have conquered

empires, invented the most amazing inventions, explored unheard of places, and achieved incredible things. Many with only a dream as currency have bought a better future for entire nations and peoples. Everyone has a dream. Perhaps it is unspoken, unexplained, and maybe even unrealized, but it is there—or at least it was.

The Death of a Dream

The day Jesus Christ was crucified, we can guess that the dreams of thousands must have been crushed. Only that could really explain the incredible anger and fury that they levied against him that day. What would make a crowd go from shouting and dancing in the street a few days before, as Jesus arrived in the city, to demanding his death sentence only a few days later? Utter despair: absolute hopelessness and disappointment. They had believed him. They had an idea of how he would come and what he would do. When he arrived, boldly confronting the corrupt religious system, performing miracles, and cleansing the temple, his followers bought in—and they bought in completely.

> When he arrived, boldly confronting the corrupt religious system, performing miracles, and cleansing the temple, his followers bought in— and they bought in completely.

No doubt when Jesus emerged from obscurity into his public ministry, a dream emerged alongside his popularity. It was the dream of a liberated and empowered Israel, a dream of freedom and blessing, a dream whose torch burned brightly in the hearts of thousands of oppressed Jews.

The Jewish people had borne the brunt of a variety of invaders' occupations through the centuries. These people's imaginations burned with passion for a day when the Messiah would come and lift the heavy yoke of oppression and fulfill the prophets' predictions that called for the "acceptable year of the Lord."

To those who were aware of the proceedings—in many ways, very secret proceedings—going on in the inner halls of power that Friday morning, the news that Jesus had been arrested and that he was about to stand trial must have been unbelievable. And when they saw him beaten, wounded, and bound, the same anticipation that had caused them to celebrate his coming and had elevated their hopes to a frenzy of excitement now turned to anger and scorn; to contempt for one, who in their minds, had undoubtedly duped them, conned them, and most importantly disappointed them. The rage that disappointment can generate can boggle the mind. They must have been so disappointed.

But they had gotten it wrong from the beginning. They had not heard what he had said. They had been deafened by their own anticipation and frustration. Their pent-up desperation had caused them to hear what they wanted to hear, not what he actually said. He did not come to rule but to die. He had not come to be served but to serve. He had not come to receive the payment demanded by justice but rather to pay it. He had come to pay the debt owed by man.

> But they had gotten it wrong from the beginning. They had not heard what he had said. They had been deafened by their own anticipation and frustration.

But in great contrast, the people had to have been so disappointed; the dreams of so many who had embraced his ministry and his identity were dashed. There is nothing so painful as the death of a dream.

While we are often so hard on the people connected to the Lord's crucifixion, we don't realize we are more like them than we would like to admit. Often we, too, become angry and frustrated when our dreams don't turn out exactly the way we thought they would. We also can miss God's plan for our lives when we flavor God's purposes with our own thoughts and expectations of how things should be. Our own ambitions, egos, and self-centered ideas must be destroyed for the pure purposes of God to be accomplished in our lives. We must deal with our "me, myself, and I" complexes. They are deceivers, manipulators, and thieves. These facades will cause us to process every event in our lives through a self-serving lens. Instead of allowing us to learn the lessons of sacrifice and endurance that we may become strong and effective, they will cause us to seek only for our convenience and comfort, often at the expense of the will of the Father and of our true destiny.

> Our own ambitions, egos, and self-centered ideas must be destroyed for the pure purposes of God to be accomplished in our lives.

In my life and my own pilgrimage into my destiny, I've had to deal with the pain that comes as a result of the death of certain personal ambitions and dreams. These dreams were so filled with my own ambitions and unreasonable expectations that their demises were among the darkest moments of my life—and I thank God for them all. Because through them I learned that my life could even become greater than the limitations of my own ambitions.

Our carnal dreams will always sell us out in the end. They will always limit our potential to our own abilities and, as a result, top us out so far below the level of divine potential that God has planned for us. Thus our fleshly dreams and ambitions must be nailed to the cross and killed if we are to be truly effective in God's kingdom. But this death of your dream is not the final word on your potential. It is, rather, the removal of the natural barriers to the working of the supernatural in your life.

As we visit Calvary and there bear our crosses, we must not get hung up. The cross is a necessary stop on the road to your destiny, but it is not your final destiny. It is only a place of purification, a place where the flesh is set aside for a greater good. But if we are not careful, we can get locked in a time warp of pain and hurt and begin to think that our cross must be carried our whole lives. Certainly, life will always have challenges, but I have known people who should have already reached their Pentecost, their destinies, but are still carrying some cross of affliction and struggle. Even for Jesus, enduring the cross was only for a brief moment in time and not forever. Visit Calvary you must. But you also must not get stuck there. You must come to your Calvary and then move on.

God is the giver of dreams and visions, but they must be purified on the altar of sacrifice for them to become lasting, loving, and life-giving. No wonder Jesus said, "If any man comes after me let him deny himself, take up his cross and follow me." Don't be afraid to see your dreams crucified. Commend them into the hands of the Father and let them go. Those that were from him will return to live again, free from the threat of "self" sabotage. And those that don't were never meant to be anyway, and were simply a distraction designed to interrupt the flow of God's purposes for your life.

> Don't be afraid to see your dreams crucified. Commend them into the hands of the Father and let them go.

Impact Points

1. **Your dream is a gift from God.** God gave each of us the capacity to dream when he created us. It's one of our most divine qualities.

   Proverbs 13:12: "Hope deferred makes the heart sick, but when the desire comes, it is a tree of life."

2. **Unrealized expectations lead to disappointment and usually result in high levels of frustration and anger.**

   Luke 23:20, 21: "Pilate, therefore, wishing to release Jesus, again called out to them. But they shouted, saying, 'Crucify Him, Crucify Him!'"

3. **God is the giver of dreams and visions, but they must be purified**

first. They need purifying on the altar of sacrifice for them to become lasting, loving, and life-giving.

Luke 23:46: "And when Jesus had cried out with a loud voice, He said, 'Father, into Your hands I commit My spirit.' Having said this Hhe breathed His last."

For Group Discussion or Self-Reflection:

1. Imagine for a moment what ways you can transform your dreams and desires into opportunities to serve others for a greater good than what you had imagined. Discuss or write about these transformations.

2. Sacrifice teaches us the valuable lessons of selflessness. Dreams that haven't been tested with suffering are often too self-serving to be of any lasting value. What was the greatest "dream" disappointment of your life? Describe the feelings that followed.

Coaching for Success

A dream is hope with pictures. Everything that exists began as a dream. We are never more like God than when we dream. Today, unleash your creative potential and dream. Swing for the fences! Pull off the limits and fire up the engines of your imagination, and even list a few of your dreams for good measure, no matter how unlikely they seem. Be careful not to listen to the voice of reason. Reason has its purpose and its place, but it is water to the creative fires of the imagination.

When dreams don't work out, we're left dealing with disappointment

. . .

Jesus' arrest, trial, and crucifixion caused tremendous disappointment among the Jewish masses who longed for the Messiah to come. This disappointment led to the frenzy of anger that they exhibited toward Jesus during his passion, but their expectations were not realistic, they were not balanced. Often our expectations are built on inaccurate assumptions or untruths. Like the people of Jesus' day, we can be devastated when our dreams don't materialize. Healthy expectations come from accurate information and well-developed processing faculties, both mental and spiritual. These faculties, when based on good information, can produce a maturity that helps us maintain balance. Seek to dream without reason and without limitation, but plan and act from a position of maturity.

We must be willing to see our dreams nailed to the Cross and killed if we are to truly become effective in God's kingdom. The cross is a necessary stop on the road to our destiny. Don't grieve too long. Commend your dreams into the hands of the Father and let them go. Give them a few days. If they are from him, he will breathe life into them again.

Prayer of Reflection

Lord, my dreams are so dear to me. They spring from the deepest part of my soul. But today I am willing to lay them at your feet, to allow them to be nailed to the cross so that I might be conformed to your image. Test my dreams, Lord, by your sacrifice and wash them with your blood until they are no longer filled with my personal interests, but by your kingdom will.

Chapter Ten

THE RESURRECTION OF
A VISION

Key Text: Mark 16:9: "Now when He arose early on the first day of the week, He appeared first to Mary Magdalene, out of whom He had cast seven demons."

Jesus' idea of destiny is so different from ours most of the time. And that is a good thing. I must say, if I were Jesus Christ and had just experienced what he experienced during his torture and death on the cross, I would have done the resurrection a little differently. I mean, if I had been betrayed by a friend, abandoned by the rest, spit upon, cursed, lied about, severely beaten, and crucified, when I came out of the grave I would have made a few more unscheduled visits than he did, if you know what I mean. And they would have been to a select group of people who had a celestial visit coming. I probably would have made another midnight visit to the palace of Caiaphas, saying, "Guess who?"; or maybe appeared to the Sanhedrin in the Hall of Hewn Stones; or perhaps shown up in Pilate's courtroom, saying, "I'm back." But not Jesus. No, he understood destiny and had

> He was clear about his purpose for coming into the world. It was for those very people who did what they did to him that he came to die.

no identity crisis, no need to get even. He was clear about his purpose for coming into the world. It was for those very people who did what they did to him that he came to die.

King of Misfits

So instead of making a grand appearance at some strategic location in an "I'll-get-you-back"–kind of visit, Jesus makes his first appearance to a woman, previously demonized, in an obscure garden outside the busy commerce center of Jerusalem (John 20, the appearance to Mary Magdalene). She had been delivered by Jesus only in the last couple of years, and now he grants her the grand privilege of becoming the first evangelist of the New Covenant. Jesus sent her to tell the apostles, who were currently hiding for their lives (those great men of faith and power), about the resurrection.

By doing so he offers hope to all of us who have fallen, been bound, and humiliated by sin. Yes, the very first appearance of the resurrected Christ was to a woman with a past, a woman whose life had been transformed, who had become a woman of light because of the victory he had won.

For Mary, coming to the tomb that early on the third day had more to do with loyalty than with faith. Reading the text of the Gospels, it is quite clear that her visit was all about love for the Lord and a personal commitment that she felt toward him. She was no quitter. And she had not forgotten what Jesus had done for her. Besides,

> Besides, she was a misfit and an outcast from society. She was not concerned about the opinions of men and had long since lost the fear of social rejection or of losing her life.

she was a misfit and an outcast from society. She was not concerned about the opinions of men and had long since lost the fear of social rejection or of losing her life. She had proven that when she stood at the foot of the cross, by staying when almost everyone else had abandoned him. No, she was not afraid; she was devastated! All she could think about was what life was like before he came.

For her, prior to Jesus' coming, life had been a living hell. She had fallen so far into the pit of rejection and despair that her spiritual freedom and free will had been surrendered to the devil, and with it her morals and decency. In Jesus she had found freedom and peace where, in others, she had only found judgment and condemnation. When he looked at her, all he could see through the eyes of love was a confused, abused daughter that had become a slave to sin. She was the epitome of what he had come to do. So with the gentleness of a loving father, he had freed her and restored her without judgment or condemnation.

> In Jesus she had found freedom and peace where, in others, she had only found judgment and condemnation.

Hope Lives . . .

Jesus' appearance to Mary in the garden that resurrection morning must have been a vote of confidence and affirmation for her, to say the least. For one who had been so devastated, humiliated, even captivated by hell and sin, it really underscored the point and power of the resurrection. What a fitting way to introduce this new kingdom initiative, and to declare to the principalities and powers of this earth that death, hell and the grave had been defeated. To choose one who once was a slave to the flesh and to the devil was a powerful sign of victory and an appropriate message announcing the intentions of Christ's kingdom and what was to come for the kingdom of darkness.

Now with the cross behind and the resurrection having been accomplished, the ground rules had been completely redefined. No longer would death rule the hearts of mankind through fear, for it had been defeated. No longer would the dreams and destinies of people be dashed by the grim reality of sin and despair. No, with the victory of the resurrection came the hope of success and personal fulfillment in life and eternity. Death was no longer the master and we its fearful subjects, but rather we were freed to become what God had purposed us to become. We were loosed from the power of the flesh to rule over us and limit our potential through a paradigm of fear.

> Death was no longer the master and we its fearful subjects, but rather we were freed to become what God had purposed us to become.

The door into the favor of God, the way of access into the presence of the Lord that Adam and Eve had enjoyed before sin slammed it shut, had been reopened by Christ on the cross. And now we, as soldiers of the cross, without the condemnation of sin, could attack the kingdom of the god of this world with faith as our focus instead of fear, joy as our anthem, and love and acceptance as our banner.

There are moments when our dreams seem to go up in a puff of smoke, when our hopes are mortally wounded by the vicious mobs of the disappointed.

When this happens, give it a little while. Let it rest maybe three days or so, then go back to where you laid your dreams and let the Resurrection and the Life restore, commission, and renew your vision. He will give you a vision that even death itself cannot take away.

Impact Points

1. **Jesus understood destiny and his mission and purpose.** Coming to grips with who you are and what God has called you to do is the surest formula for achieving your destiny. Be completely at peace with what God has called you to do and the destiny he has planned for you.

   Luke 24:25, 26: "Oh foolish ones, and slow of heart to believe in all the prophets have spoken! Ought not the Christ to have suffered these things and to enter into His glory?"

2. **At the resurrection, Jesus made new life and a fresh start available to all who have been devastated by sin.** This point is made clear by his appearing first to Mary following his resurrection. She had been so victimized and bound by the devil and enslaved in her present by the shackles of her past. Being the first to see Jesus after his death was no doubt a vote of confidence for her and one that resonates with all of us who have been a puppet in sin's grip. No matter where you have been, what you have done, or what has been done to you, don't be afraid to dream again. A living Jesus has given you the opportunity to pursue your destiny.

John 20:31: "But these are written that you may believe that Jesus is the Christ, the Son of God, and that believing you may have life in His name."

3. **Death need no longer control us through fear.** Fear is one of the most powerful threats to your destiny. Failure, defeat, humiliation, and the like are all by-products of the fear of death. But through the power of the resurrection, we can now dream and achieve without the constant fear of failure.

1 John 4:18: "There is no fear in love; but perfect love casts out fear, because fear involves torment. But he who fears has not been made perfect in love."

Question for Group Discussion or Self-Reflection

The fear of death and failure can hold us all out of our purpose if we allow it. Take a moment and list several common fears that war against your potential. Now take them to God in prayer.

Coaching for Success

Faith is the key to overcoming fear. Fear and faith cannot work together. One will ultimately gain control of your life and consequently your future. Fear must be confronted, challenged, and overcome. Both fear and faith operate in a similar manner—the expectation of an anticipated end. Therefore, study the promises of God to his children and learn to speak your agreement with those promises over your life situations. Focus on his word, not your circumstances, and trust God for what is best concerning you.

Prayer of Reflection

Lord Jesus, you control and hold my destiny in the palm of your hand. You proved by your resurrection and compassion for those bound by sin and shame that I, too, can be forgiven and used for your glory. You are the victorious prince of life. Your victory over death, hell, and the grave was complete. Therefore, I am free to live again, to dream, to hope. I thank you greatly for this simple truth.

Chapter Eleven

THE REVELATION OF A MISSION

Key Text: Matthew 28:10: "Then Jesus said to them, 'Do not be afraid. Go and tell My brethren to go to Galilee, and there they will see Me.'"

Epiphany is a word that describes a moment of enlightenment, a revelation, a moment when the light goes on and understanding is achieved. Educators look for it. Inventors live for it. Musicians are on a continual quest for it. An epiphany moment is when what has been unclear, misunderstood, without harmony, or has been kept in secret is finally revealed. What a discovery! What a feeling!

> An epiphany moment is when what has been unclear, misunderstood, without harmony, or has been kept in secret is finally revealed. What a discovery! What a feeling!

Working with leadership groups through the years, I came to understand early on that if a leader is to have success in developing a team, and to be effective in casting a vision and a mission for that team, there must be a moment of epiphany. There must be a moment when the light comes on and each individual "gets it." It will most certainly come at different moments and through different means. But it must come.

Knowledge without revelation is nothing more than mere matter in motion. But add a clear revelation and you have conviction. It is an element that must not be taken for granted. For in its presence a fact becomes a truth and an idea becomes a principle. It produces a cause with force inside. It brings power with it. It can produce a cause for which to live, and, if necessary, for which to die.

Jesus knew that. He knew that if he was to leave the destiny of the church in the hands of common people like you and me, it would require a revelation. It would require an impartation. So before he could send his disciples to Jerusalem to receive power, he must send them to Galilee to receive revelation. Power without understanding will always produce confusion.

> This meeting would become an extended time of explanation and revelation. Even after the resurrection, the disciples still did not get it. They were, in many ways, still in the dark.

When we harmonize the Gospels we find that after Jesus was resurrected, he sent his disciples into the region of Galilee to await his arrival there (Matthew 28:10). This meeting would become an extended time of explanation and revelation. Even after the resurrection, the disciples still did not get it. They were, in many ways, still in the dark as to the plan of God and what had been accomplished on the cross and through the resurrection.

They were in the dark partly because of their own shame. They couldn't have been feeling very good about themselves at this time. I am sure that their emotions were confused as well as being ashamed of their actions during the trauma of Jesus' trial and execution. And now that he had risen, they were overjoyed at his appearing, but felt even worse about themselves. What would Jesus do to them? How would he relate to his leadership team, who had just blown it so badly?

The answer to this question comes after they have migrated to Galilee and gone back to work—back to fishing. (It was Peter, their leader, who had initiated this grand excursion to go back to their dirty, heavy nets.) It is early one morning when Jesus appears on the shore after they have fished all night and caught nothing. He invites them, once again, to do things his way and, of course, they experience a great catch of fish. Then he invites them for breakfast. It is time for their first "post-failure leadership meeting," a performance review of sorts. They brace themselves. Here it comes. At least an "I told you so"—or maybe even worse.

An Invitation to Restoration

It is during this encounter that I am awed by the leadership style of Jesus. He feeds them and encourages them and never even mentions their failure. Never *mentions* it. Instead, he cuts right to the heart of the matter with the one who was the king of failure, Peter. The one who had lied about him, cursed, and even swore to God that he did not know him. And Jesus' word to this man was an invitation to restoration. Restoration, it seems, always leads to fresh revelation.

> He invites them, once again, to do things his way and, of course, they experience a great catch of fish.

"Peter, if you love me, feed my sheep." I would imagine that Peter was quite taken back by this. "What did you say Lord?" he might have said. "It sounds like an invitation back into ministry. Have you forgotten what I did? What I said? . . . You of all people should know that I can't come back. I'm disqualified. I'm a quitter, a loser, a coward in the first degree."

But Jesus' response was simply to say again: "Peter, if you love me, feed my sheep."

It had been necessary that Jesus take them to a private location, where he could explain the events of his life, death, and resurrection in light of the Old Testament.

It would be easy for us to get a little judgmental toward the disciples at this point, but it was not so much about unbelief as it was about misunderstanding. They could not deny that Jesus was alive. He clearly was. The question was, "What does it all mean?"

Sometimes, making sense of it all is half the battle. Even in our lives, when we have been through a similar pattern regarding our own destinies and dreams—and we all have—it takes a little while, maybe even a seminar with the resurrected Lord, who can bring a revelation to our thinking so that we can understand the plan of God and why things happened the way they did.

Jesus, during this extended time together, was able to explain to them the whole story from the beginning. *Luke writes (Luke 24:44-49) that he discussed how the Law and Prophets and even the Psalms spoke concerning him and his mission to earth. Can you imagine what it would have been like to have been part of this class?* What an opportunity it must have been to hear God explain his intentions and the accomplishments of redemption to those eager ears.

For example, he may well have explained that the blood of a spotless lamb could never take away the sin of a man, but rather that the lamb represented a sinless Man who could; that the scapegoat could never banish the sin of the nation of Israel, but rather represented the Man who would carry away the sins of a new nation, a nation of redeemed people, whose king would buy their freedom with his own blood.

There had to be understanding and clarification before there could be an acceptance of the mission that would become their life's work and the purpose and the mission of the church. So powerful was this time together that almost all of them would eventually die for the truths that were communicated and clarified during this forty-day seminar. And not one would recant or deny the reality of what they had learned there.

After Jesus explained it all again, Luke says that he opened their understanding that they might comprehend the Scriptures (Luke 24:45). As he gave them revelation, suddenly it all made perfect sense. With this new enlightenment, now they could see him everywhere in the Old Testament: in the tabernacle, the priesthood, the temple, and yes, of course, in the feast, and in the wilderness.

Revelation will always precede a new mission, a new level of authority, a new season of responsibility. Therefore, equipped with this divinely released revelation, they were now ready to receive their mission and purpose.

With complete understanding they would be able to defend their faith in a hostile social system and world. Their faith, based upon their understanding of the purposes of God in Christ, would become the foundation of fulfillment of their mission.

> With this new enlightenment, now they could see him everywhere in the Old Testament: in the tabernacle, the priesthood, the temple, and yes, of course, in the feast, and in the wilderness.

Their mission would be to "Go into all the world and preach the Gospel [Good News] to every creature" (Mark 16:15). It would be to "Make disciples of all nations . . . Teaching them to observe all things that I have commanded you" (Matthew 28:19, 20). To accomplish this objective they must have a revelation and be able to bounce back from the greatest trauma of their lives, the events of the Jerusalem experience.

And so do we. A fresh revelation is the price of passage into your future, especially after you have been traumatized by failure. Those Jerusalem moments—the garden, the rejection by the religious, the misunderstanding of the world, the death of their dream—each event had to be processed and put in its place so that those who had experienced them could move on.

The disciples had to understand those moments as part of a divine plan to accomplish God's purpose in Christ. They had not been misled or deceived. Even their failures fit into the plan. God did have a destiny for them all, and this plan was never out of control. Rather, God was calling the shots at each moment, even the uncomfortable ones. As a result they would never be the same again.

I guess now they also were not as likely to judge others and their failures. There is something very humbling about being broken by your own weaknesses. When revelation comes, and with it a proper perspective, that healing can position a leader for greatness.

After the Lord opened their eyes and demonstrated his love for them in spite of their failures, it brought a new perspective to their thinking. From this new perspective they could forgive themselves and see the light of destiny through the dark clouds of despair. They finally understood. With this revelation came the realization that there was work to be done.

But Jesus also said there was still a part that must be completed. You need power, he was saying: Go back to Jerusalem.

> After the Lord opened their eyes and demonstrated his love for them in spite of their failures, it brought a new perspective to their thinking.

Impact Points

1. **There is nothing as humbling as being broken by your own weaknesses.** While the disciples were no doubt thrilled that Jesus was alive, they must have felt great shame and disappointment toward themselves. They had walked out on him when he needed them the most.

   Matthew 6:12: "And forgive us our debts, as we forgive our debtors."

2. **Knowledge without revelation is powerless to effect change.** But add revelation to knowledge and you develop a conviction with authority. People respond not just to our knowledge, but to spiritual authority as well. When seeking your destiny, ask God for a clear revelation and you will find the authority to accomplish your purpose.

   Luke 24:45: "And He opened their understanding, that they might comprehend the Scriptures."

3. **Power without understanding will always produce confusion.** Confusion is not the ground upon which a firm future can be built. Before you seek power, seek understanding. Wisdom will make the power of our anointing purposeful and productive.

Proverbs 16:16: "How much better to get wisdom than gold! And to get understanding is to be chosen rather than silver."

4. **Restoration often leads to a revelation moment.** Revelation will always precede a new mission, a new level of authority, and a new season of responsibility. Accountability is always connected to our level of revelation. When we know and have understanding, we are ready to accept the commission to an important mission.

John 21:15: "Simon, son of Jonah, do you love Me more than these? . . . Feed my lambs."

For Group Discussion or Self-Reflection

Have you ever let someone down? Remember how that felt, knowing that you had caused them pain? Take a moment and revisit those emotions.

Forgiveness is such a beautiful thing. Now that you have revisited the feelings of guilt associated with your failure, remember that Jesus never accused his disciples or focused on their mistakes. He won't yours, either. His attention was given to restoration. Peace is the place where you can thrive, succeed, and achieve. Make peace with your past today! Forgive yourself. Jesus already has! Now forgive others who have harmed you in like manner.

Take some time to reflect on these truths.

Coaching for Success

Failure usually leaves us in a daze, a fog. It can leave us without clear direction and purpose. In the aftermath of a failure, disappointment can blind us to our destiny and potential opportunities. But when offered restoration without condemnation and shame, we can again find our way with clarity and purpose. To offer restoration is to allow us to begin at least where we were before we failed. It also promises hope that we can proceed toward our destiny without shame or guilt.

This week offer restoration to someone in your world who needs to be restored! It will release them to dream again.

Allow God to restore you as you begin to focus again on your dreams.

Prayer of Reflection

Lord, you know me. You know my weakness and frailties all too well. You are intimately acquainted with my motives. I cannot hide from you. Yet you still call me to your side, to stand in your service. Thank you for your confidence in me even when I have none in myself. Please give me understanding and wisdom. Let me know your purpose and vision for my life so that I may enter my future without fear and bring honor to your name even though I am challenged by my past. You are the God of revelation.

Chapter Twelve

THE REALIZATION OF A DESTINY

Key Text: Luke 24:49: "Behold, I send the Promise of My Father upon you; but tarry in the city of Jerusalem until you are endued with power from on high."

The Promise of the Father . . .

For years I, like so many others in "Full Gospel" circles, really failed to understand what it meant when Jesus told his disciples to return to Jerusalem and wait until they received the "Promise of the Father." We knew about the "power" part, certainly the tongues, and even the idea of becoming a witness, but we had little comprehension of how the "Promise of the Father" was connected to the overall covenant plan of redemption.

The Promise of the Father is really God's Promise to reconcile and redeem man from his fallen state and sin-devastated condition that came as a result of his disobedience in the garden. It is the promise of another man, a second Adam, who would do what the first Adam failed to do.

The promise of man's redemption from the effects of the fall could literally be traced back to the beginning. It was prophesied by God himself in the garden after the fall of man, and reiterated by him through a definite sequence of events and activities throughout history—events that ultimately culminated in the coming of Jesus Christ.

We cannot separate the coming of the Christ from the coming of the promise of the Father. They are intricately connected and streamed together through the promises of Abraham, the role of Moses in giving the law of the Covenant, even the purpose of the nation of Israel. When you view them as a whole instead of a group of unrelated people and events, a picture comes into view that can explain God's purpose and bring a revelation that will indeed release power in the life of the believer. For they all tell the same story, our story; the story of how we were lost but now we have been found, of how we lost our rights as heirs, yet through Christ have regained our inheritance in his kingdom.

Perhaps it would help to think of all of these people and events of biblical history as a road leading to a common destination point. And that common destination point was not the Cross or the empty tomb, but rather the birthing point of a new race of humanity that would be called the body of Christ—the church. This birthing point would be Jerusalem on the day of Pentecost.

After much study and thought I came to believe that the Pentecostal event that took place following the Messiah's ascension back to Heaven was a key component to the whole story line of redemption. You might say that it was the climax, the grand finale. Now, I certainly do not seek to diminish the centrality of the Cross in redemption. *It is indeed the price that was paid* and it cannot be underestimated. And without the resurrection we would have no hope of victory over death, hell, and the grave. *It is the power that was produced.* But too often we stop our celebration and study of redemption at the resurrection instead of moving further up the road a few days to the Day of Pentecost. Pentecost was the purpose that redemption achieved.

I believe that the reason we tend to stop short of including this event in our concept of redemption is because of our tendency in modern theological paradigms to try to compartmentalize everything. It seems easier to understand if we can divide and define each subject independently of everything else. So we have people who specialize in Covenant theology and others in soteriology; those who focus on eschatology and still others who study any one of a number of other "ologies." But one of the great liabilities of this exclusive thinking is that we can miss the divine links that connect each of these disciplines with the other, and in doing so miss the most mature revelation of God's overall purpose for man. This purpose is miraculously streamed through each area of study. So we keep dividing what God is uniting and continue to split our thoughts in an attempt to understand a God whose primary purpose is to reconcile all things into one (Colossians 1:19).

> But one of the great liabilities of this exclusive thinking is that we can miss the divine links that connect each of these disciplines with the other, and in doing so miss the most mature revelation of God's overall purpose for man.

Now I'm not saying that these specializations are not helpful, even necessary. But I am saying that we must also look at the big picture and constantly measure our individual study in a particular area against a singular foundational reality. That reality is the redemption of man.

The truth is the whole story, the entire book, every arena and endeavor of theological study must be properly interpreted and applied in the context of redemption. Each of the Old Testament characters and events can only be properly understood against the background of God's redemptive purpose for man in Christ. Jesus Christ would come as a man, the promised seed of the woman, and of Abraham, and would crush Satan's head of authority and dominion and take back all that was lost by man in the fall. God's agenda regarding man after the fall was to reconcile him to himself, to his rightful position of authority and responsibility as God's agent ruler of the earth.

Therefore, all of the events and characters of the Old Testament are leading to the introduction of this one seed who would become the central figure of redemption, the man Jesus Christ. He, as the second Adam, would be the summation of every theological thought and previous message from God to man, and on the Day of Pentecost the whole movement would be distilled into one glorious moment of inheritance. It was absolutely necessary for those who would constitute the first church to be present and witness the moment. They had to be included in the outpouring. But Jesus first had to get the disciples from Galilee back to Jerusalem and back to the temple for the Day of Pentecost.

> It was absolutely necessary for those who would constitute the first church to be present and witness the moment.

From Galilee to Jerusalem

I have made the trip from Galilee to Jerusalem. It is a hard, uphill journey over desert terrain and mountains, a real wilderness in the biblical sense. In ancient times it was not only exhausting but also dangerous. Remember the story of the Good Samaritan? While he was not traveling to, but away from, Jerusalem (toward Jericho), it was still the same general route. It was infested with bandits and highwaymen. On foot, it was a ten-day journey, and hard days at that. But I would imagine that as the disciples made their trip from Galilee back to Jerusalem, little thought was given to bandits or the strenuous climb. No, this must have been a journey filled with incredible emotion.

Conversations while en route must have been a mixture of discussions about what had happened before they left and what might happen upon their return. I'm sure they shared moments of wonder reminiscing about

PILGRIMAGE TO PENTECOST | 143

some of the miracles Jesus performed and lessons he had taught there. They probably shared a laugh or two about how Jesus had confronted the Pharisees in the temple and the look of shock on their faces as he fashioned a whip and ran them out of there. And I'm sure there were more private moments when their thoughts were ravaged with regrets. Regrets over how they had behaved during the Lord's passion, how they had run out on him at the very moment he had needed them most.

As they traveled I'm sure you could have heard them discussing the situation, saying things like, "Our Lord must have very good reasons for sending us back, but it's going to be risky, isn't it?" And, "What if they see us?" And, "I know it is Pentecost. Maybe we can get lost in the crowd." Another would chime in, "Perhaps there is some connection between the promise of the Father, being endued with the power that Jesus talked about, and the Pentecost festival?" These questions must have been in the forefront of their minds. I mean, forty days ago they were forced to flee from Jerusalem for their lives. And now they are being sent back? This must have produced great anxiety. What could Jesus have in mind sending them back to such a place and at such a time?

> I mean, forty days ago they were forced to flee from Jerusalem for their lives. And now they are being sent back? This must have produced great anxiety.

Why Jerusalem?

In this story I have found three lessons about destiny that I have used to coach and encourage Christians over the years. And they are lessons that the disciples must also have discovered as they were being sent back to Jerusalem by Jesus. These, like most of destiny's lessons, rest quietly in the background of the circumstances of our lives.

Lesson 1: *Often the key to our destiny resides in the place of our*

greatest personal failure. For the disciples, Jerusalem was just such a place. Only forty days before they had abandoned Jesus and scattered, driven away by their fear of the personal price their identities as his disciples might demand. And being unwilling to pay the price, they fled from their responsibilities and their commitments and lost themselves in a moment of disgrace. Going back to Jerusalem, in a way, allowed them to confront their failure and convert the dishonor associated with that failure into an understanding of forgiveness and hope. For us to realize our destiny, we, as they, must make peace with our past. We must afford ourselves the opportunity to replace the moments of failure in our lives with the same forgiveness and hope that they must have found upon their return to Jerusalem on the Day of Pentecost. The link to our future, the link to our destiny, is almost always associated with settling the issues connected to the failures of our past. And it is not unusual to have to return to the "scene of the crime" to gain the perspectives and closure we need to move on and discover the real potential for our life that God has planned.

Lesson 2: *Great risk is frequently a hallmark of a destiny moment.* When the disciples of Jesus returned to Jerusalem, they must have understood the risk associated with their return. They must have believed they were wanted men, that there was a price on their heads. The same fear that caused them to abandon Jesus at the crucifixion must have pressured them to play it safe and contemplate thoroughly the possibilities and dangers involved in returning to Jerusalem so soon after the events of Christ's death. Had they yielded to that fear and refused to return to Jerusalem, they would have missed the greatest destiny moment of their lives and would have been deprived of the power and provision it afforded.

Fear is the enemy of us all. That personal instinct to survive can lead us away from our places of destiny. It seems that one of the common characters cast in the drama of destiny is the intimidating, relentless fear of losing what we have in pursuit of what we desire. But every great leader can attest to the fact that the enemy, fear, must be confronted and defeated.

Risk is what stands between the mundane and the extraordinary, between good and great, between fear and faith. Every person in successful pursuit of his or her destiny must visit Jerusalem and be willing to risk it all. Don't be surprised if your destiny is waiting on the other side of your greatest personal risk.

Lesson 3: *Jerusalem was the place of their greatest potential. It was the logical place for God to announce the birth of the church and the victory of Christ over death, hell, and the grave.* During this Feast of Pentecost, scores of thousands of people from virtually every known nation of the world could personally witness the spectacular manifestation of God's declaration of victory through Christ. Therefore, the disciples who had been commissioned by Christ to go into all the world with the good news of the resurrection would commence this mission with the assistance of the Holy Spirit. Without a publicist or an advertising agency, the good news of the Gospel would spread like wildfire through flash points of revelation carried in the hearts of all those who witnessed the events of that day in Jerusalem. Yes, for the disciples Jerusalem was indeed a place of past failure and incredible risk, but it was also undeniably the place where a ripe field ready for harvest would be reaped; it would produce the seed for a global harvest that continues to this day. It was truly the place of their greatest potential.

> Risk is what stands between the mundane and the extraordinary, between good and great, between fear and faith.

Why the Feast of Pentecost?

Without a doubt each of the rituals, services, and celebrations of ancient Israel's history contained veiled truths and hidden spiritual realities. We serve a God who does nothing by accident, but instead, with masterful, meticulous planning designs his strategies for our lives. Interwoven throughout the entire Old Testament is the veiled story of a coming nation of spiritual sons and daughters called the church. The emergence of the church would represent the culmination of God's entire redemptive purpose and plan for man. You see, it was God's purpose to unify all things in Christ, both things in heaven and things on earth. On the day of Pentecost a new race of people, a holy family of God, would step from the pages of the Torah and ranks of the Jews to become a new people consisting of not only Jews but also "all that are afar off, everyone whom the Lord our God calls to Him" (Acts 2:39).

> Interwoven throughout the entire Old Testament is the veiled story of a coming nation of spiritual sons and daughters called the church.

This new family would have as its head a living Lord who was in the beginning with God, became a man in the flesh, lived among us as a man without sin, died an undeserved sinner's death, and had been raised to life again because death could not hold him. It had no righteous claim on him. This was none other than Jesus Christ.

God was about to join in one body all those who had been separated by the Old Covenant and make one new man in Christ Jesus. There would be a sudden moment during this Feast of Pentecost that would become the moment of genesis, a moment of new creation and new beginnings, a declaration of restoration throughout the universe for all that the first Adam had lost through the fall.

At Pentecost, a ragtag mob would become a movement overnight. It would be that, in this sudden moment, an unusual mixture of people who had no natural affinity would become a holy family—true joint heirs. They were priests and ex-prostitutes, fishermen and farmers, tax collectors and military men, businessmen and women, housewives young and old, people from all walks of life. This event would galvanize a new movement, define a new reality for living, and introduce the beginning of the end of the ages with the church as God's witness declaring his grace and desire to reach fallen man.

Pentecost had been celebrated for generations. This, the first post-resurrection Pentecost, would be the long-awaited reality for which all other Pentecost feasts prior to it were but a mere shadow. Pentecost was the celebration of firstfruits and it is indeed fitting that the first fruits of an end-time harvest and the introduction of a new order of existence and restored relationship between God and man would have its beginning in Jerusalem during the Feast of Pentecost.

> They were priests and ex-prostitutes, fishermen and farmers, tax collectors and military men, businessmen and women, housewives young and old, people from all walks of life.

Yes, it would be launched from Jerusalem, but it would not stop there. And it has not stopped yet, and will not stop until it has reached the ends of the earth. That is what Jesus predicted. He said that it would begin in Jerusalem, spread to Judea, Samaria, and to the uttermost parts of the world. Samaria was probably included, specifically, as a reminder for all of us who are misfits and rejected by mainstream religion that we will not be left out. It reminds us that all of the fragmented human race must be reached with the news that we are wanted, important, and sought after by God, that we are welcome in the family of faith.

Ironically, the Jews believed that the Feast of Pentecost also coincided with the giving of the Law at Mount Sinai, which they believed happened fifty days after Passover. It, too, was accompanied by the presence of fire and wind as signs of the manifest presence of God.

In a way, Pentecost does represent the giving of a new Law. It would be the law of a new kingdom, a kingdom whose laws brought liberty instead of condemnation. Pentecost represents and fulfills the prophetic utterance of the day that would come when God would engrave his law upon our hearts.

"For this is the covenant that I will make with the house of Israel

> Pentecost represents and fulfills the prophetic utterance of the day that would come when God would engrave his law upon our hearts.

after those days, says the Lord: I will put my laws in their mind and write them on their hearts; and I will be their God, and they shall be My people" (Hebrews 8:10 quoting Jeremiah 31:31-33).

The purpose of God at Pentecost was to birth a new race of men and to ignite a powerful force in the earth, a force for change, a force that would define a new reality, a "kingdom reality" on earth via this new race of sons and daughters of God called the church. For this purpose to be effective and to reach its greatest potential, it must be revealed in such a way that in one sweeping movement, the reality of the resurrection—the undeniable power and majesty which God worked in Christ through redemption—must be made manifest before the eyes and the ears of the entire world. The only place this could be done was in Jerusalem during a festival that would draw pilgrims from virtually every nation on the earth at that time.

What a brilliant tactical move. God would use an Old Covenant religious festival attended by Jews from all over the world to announce and affirm Jesus of Nazareth as the long-awaited Messiah—and to introduce a New Covenant reality and kingdom economy. He would use the festival of firstfruits to introduce the first fruits of this new kingdom reality and the commemoration of the giving of the first law to engrave a new law upon the hearts of man.

What a moment in history. The destiny of the church was about to be realized by people who had been through an incredible pilgrimage. No, not they alone, for they have not traveled this journey alone. But they were a part, a token, and a representation of the fulfillment for those who had gone before and the firstfruits of those who would come after.

There have been many faithful travelers, destiny seekers, who, through the years, since the promise of the Father was first delivered to Abraham, have endured the struggles, crises, and trauma of change on the road to their destinies. They have each visited in their own way the same milestones and roadside stops that our Lord and the first church experienced as they made their faithful march toward Pentecost, their destiny.

> They have each visited in their own way the same milestones and roadside stops that our Lord and the first church experienced as they made their faithful march toward Pentecost, their destiny.

Impact Points

1. **Often, our destiny awaits us in the place of our greatest personal failure.** So it was with Jesus' disciples. Being sent back to Jerusalem to receive the promise of the Father (the destiny of the church) was indeed being sent back to face the greatest failure of their lives. Most had abandoned Jesus; some, even worse. Jerusalem was a key link to their complete restoration.

   Acts 1:4: "And being assembled together with them, He commanded them not to depart from Jerusalem, but to wait for the Promise of the Father, 'which,' He said, 'you have heard from Me.'"

2. **Great risk is frequently a hallmark of a destiny moment.** The disciples were not only faced with their own failure in their return to Jerusalem, but also the threat of arrest, or worse, from the same group that had crucified Jesus. They must have thought that they could be treated the same way Jesus had been. It took real courage to go back.

   Acts 2:23: "Him, being delivered by the determined purpose and foreknowledge of God, you have taken by lawless hands, have crucified, and put to death."

3. **Your destiny normally begins in the place of your greatest potential.** Jerusalem was the ideal place to ignite the Church. Pilgrims from all over the world were there and any supernatural activity was sure to be told around the world in a short time. God's wisdom would cause the fire of the new church to be carried around the world in the hearts of those who witnessed it.

Acts 2:5: "And there were dwelling in Jerusalem Jews, devout men, from every nation under heaven."

4. **At Pentecost God would create a new race of people on the Earth, called Christians.** During this time a ragtag mob would become a movement overnight. It would be the place and time when an unusual mixture of people with no natural affinity would become a holy family. It was a moment that would define the church forever.

Acts 2:41: "Then those who gladly received his word were baptized; and that day about three thousand souls were added *to them.*"

For Group Discussion or Self-Reflection

Take a moment and think about the circumstances of your life that you felt were difficult, unfair, or that came as a result of a mistake. How did you process what happened? Have you forgiven those involved, including yourself? How were you changed in the process? List several good things that happened as a result of what you went through.

Coaching for Success

Often the key to experiencing your destiny is settling the hurts and disappointments of the past. When you are being led by Jesus, you don't have to be afraid when you are sent back to the place of your past failures.

He knows that something important is waiting for you there: peace and power. The Holy Spirit will meet you there with the peace that will help heal the pain of your mistakes and the power that will propel you into your destiny. There you can forgive those who have wounded you and yourself for handling it the way that you did. This can seem risky! And consequently, this requires great courage. So be strong and courageous, knowing that your promise might be wrapped in a package marked "high risk," but that it is also marked with "great possibilities." Know this: when God sends you to a place of destiny, it may be to confront your past and it may look risky, but he will have a plan at work for healing your deepest hurts and expanding your potential in ways that you never imagined.

Prayer of Reflection

Lord, grant me the calm patience to trust you as you lead me into my destiny. Your wisdom and planning is without question superior to my own, and I know this to be true. Therefore, I believe that your purpose in my life will be fulfilled as I simply submit to your leading. I know that if I will do this, you will enlarge my capacity to a level that can contain my destiny, and I will know the joy of reaching my potential in you.

A FINAL WORD

As we have made our pilgrimage to Pentecost with Jesus and his first disciples, I hope you have come to see Pentecost from a new and expanded perspective. The way we view an event has everything to do with how we interpret its meaning, importance, and significance. As a Pentecostal leader I believe that it's fair to say that our "doctrinizing" of the Day of Pentecost has cost us much of its deeper meaning. To many of us the events of the Day of Pentecost have been reduced to a proof text in Scripture that we use to defend our particular experience. How sad is that? Because, in doing so, we miss the truly amazing part!

If I've done my job telling the Pentecost story in this book, then you have come to understand it as so much more than just a charismatic experience. It is more than just the signs and wonders of the working of the Holy Spirit, and I mean no disrespect. But rather, Pentecost was the grand destination of the journey of redemption. In a way, it was the end of something and the beginning of something better. It was the birthday of the bride of Christ, the church. I also hope that you have come to see that the story is not just about the miracle events of a first-century cultural feast in ancient Israel, but it is the story of your journey and of your experiencing your destiny as well.

We walked together through the passion of Jesus' painful moments. I know that you've seen yourself in those moments and can relate to them. And we have examined the purpose of being tested in the way that he and his disciples were tested. We now know that, though these tests are painful, we are changed through them for the better. In them we are refined, purified, and a large part of us dies—the part that needed to. And as his apostles courageously returned to Jerusalem and experienced the amazing wonder of the coming of the promise of the Father on Pentecost, so I've tried to encourage you that there yet remains a miracle appointment for you as well, when you will come to the incredible moment in your life when you experience the fulfillment of God's promise to you!

So be encouraged! Don't quit or get hung up along the way. Keep moving! Forge on ahead. Push through the passion, discover the purpose, and experience the power that only his promise can produce! Pentecost is just ahead for you!

NOTES

Chapter One

1. F. Blass and A. Debrunner, *A Greek Grammar of the New Testament and Other Early Christian Literature* (Chicago: Chicago University Press, 1975), p. 208.

2. Jos. Antiq. xiv. 13, 4; xvii. 10, 2

3. http://holylandsstudies.ag.org/blog/location-of-the-day-of-pentecost

4. A. F. Rainey and R. Steven Noltey, *The Sacred Bridge* (Jerusalem: Carta, 2006), p. 370.

Chapter Two

5. Strong's Exhaustive Concordance of the Bible: 31st Edition, Nashville, TN/New York, Abingdon Press 1973, p. 60 Greek Dictionary of the New Testament.

Chapter Three

6. Mario Murillo, *Critical Mass* (Chatsworth, California: Anthony Douglas Publishing Company, 1985), pp. 36-38.

7. Charles Colson with Ellen Santilli Vaughn, T*he Body: Being Light in Darkness* (Dallas: W Publishing Group, 1992).

Chapter Four

8. William A. Beckham, **The Second Reformation: Reshaping the Church for the 21st Century** (Houston: Touch Publications, 1995), p. 19.

9. My friend Tudor Bismark used these concepts on climate while speaking at Word Of Life Church in Tupelo, Mississippi.

10. *The American Heritage Science Dictionary* (Houghton Mifflin Company, 2005).

Chapter Six

11. Helpful information on the Passover in this chapter was taken from the International Standard Bible Encyclopedia (Grand Rapids, Michigan: William B. Eerdmans Publishing Company, 1986), pp. 675-678.

Chapter Seven

12. Albert Einstein, www.brainyquotes.com, accessed December 17, 2011, http://brainyquote.com/quotes/a/alberteinseins21993.html

13. Zvi Greenhut, "Caiaphas' Cave," *Time* magazine, August 24, 1992.

14. Uwe Siemon-Netto, "Analysis: Caiaphas—the Real Hypocrite?", United Press International, March 16, 2004.

ABOUT THE AUTHOR

For more than twenty-five years, Phillip Brassfield has served the Lord in various ministry capacities. Having been raised in a minister's home, he has been in and around the work of the Lord his entire life.

Phil was called by God at a young age to develop Christian Leaders. He has been, for many years, a trailblazer and designer of innovative and nontraditional ministry and educational concepts. He has served in almost every position imaginable in the local church including Senior Pastor, and in a variety of executive positions with three different non-traditional Christian Colleges whose primary focus was equipping leaders in partnership with the local church.

In 1997 Phil founded Destiny Ministries which has grown today into a globally recognized Apostolic Ministry committed to church planting, developing Christian Leaders and coordinating ministry efforts internationally. It also includes Destiny Leadership Institute, the division of the ministry that focuses on equipping emerging leaders through formal training and internships. He serves on the Board of Regents at Ecclesia College in Springdale, Arkansas, as a member of the Board of Directors for Churches in Covenant based in Dallas, Texas and on the Council of Elders for the Global Network of Christian Ministries, based in Houston, Texas.

He resides in the beautiful Arkansas Ozark Mountains with his wife Cathy who serves faithfully along side him in the ministry. She holds degrees in Business and Biblical Studies, and serves as a role model to countless women in ministry. She is an intercessor, and also manages the Destiny Business Office.

They are blessed with three grown children: Jordan, Drew and Drew's wife, Diana, and two Grandsons, Noah and Jonah.

Destiny Ministries Inc.
P.O. Box 341
Heber Springs, Arkansas 72543
501.887.9933
www.destinyvisioncenter.com
philbrassfield.com

Look for Phil on: Facebook and @philbrassfield on Twitter

DESTINY
PUBLICATIONS